PACESETTER

STARTER

WORKBOOK

DEREK STRANGE   DIANE HALL

OXFORD
UNIVERSITY PRESS

GW00630623

OXFORD
UNIVERSITY PRESS

Great Clarendon Street, Oxford OX2 6DP

Oxford University Press is a department of the University of Oxford.
It furthers the University's objective of excellence in research, scholarship, and education by publishing worldwide in

Oxford New York

Athens Auckland Bangkok Bogotá Buenos Aires Calcutta
Cape Town Chennai Dar es Salaam Delhi Florence Hong
Kong Istanbul Karachi Kuala Lumpur Madrid Melbourne
Mexico City Mumbai Nairobi Paris São Paulo Singapore
Taipei Tokyo Toronto Warsaw
with associated companies in Berlin Ibadan

ISBN 0-19-436326 0

1999 Impression

Printed in China

Acknowledgements

Illustrations by:
Kathy Baxendale pp 4, 12 (table headings), 15 (spot pictures), 20, 21 (chips), 26, 32, (tables), 44 63,64; Brett Breckon pp 5, 11, 12 (giraffe), 14 (mug shots), 22, 23, 31 (bedroom), 47, 53 (bus and circus), 59,73; Anna Brookes pp18 (models), 29,70; Chris Brown pp 6 (Carol & Ricky), 8 (Jack & Emma, pen & cassette), 10 (O.K Club kitchen), 17 (O.K Club members), 30 (boy), 37, 38 (boy), 41, 50,54,68; Karen Donelly pp9, 67,72; Mark Draisey pp 14 (girls on phone), 15 (ugly and handsome man), 19, 33 (robot), 35 (girl on bike etc.), 55, 61,71 Neil Gower pp3, 8 (chair, book pen etc), 16, 17 (bedroom), 21 (jeans), 31 (shapes), 35 (table headings), 38 (weather symbols), 40 (weather symbols and map), 53 (map), 65; Sharon Scotland pp 6 (4 cartoons bottom right), 10 (cartoon), 24, 40 (running, dancing), 56, 66; Tech Graphics pp 4 (map), 75; Raymond Turvey pp 18 (bedroom, shoes), 34; Katherine Walker pp 39,43,51,58, 60.

Commissioned photography by
Bill Osment pp13 ,46 (OK club members)
Paul Mulcahy pp27
Maggie Milner pp49

The Publishers would like to thank the following for their kind permission to reproduce photographs and other copyright material.

J Allan Cash p 28; Rex Features pp 4, 8 (James Bond), 18 (football, Bjorn), 61; Ronald Grant Archive pp 8 (Lisa Simpson), 18 (The Simpsons).

English you know

Dictionary work

1 a Put these words into alphabetical order (A, B, C ...).

> hamburger   bank   yacht   football   secretary
> museum   computer   video   lemonade   doctor

1 *bank*   2 *computer*   3 *doctor*   4 *football*
5 *hamburger* 6 *lemonade* 7 *museum*   8 *secretary*
9 *video*   10 *yacht*

b Put these words into alphabetical order.

> computer   cafe   cassette   cinema   coffee
> Canada   cola

1 *cafe*   2 *canada*   3 *cassette* 4 *cinema*
5 *coffe*   6 *cola*   7 *computer*

Instructions

2 Write the instructions in your language.

English	My language
Write about …	
Correct …	
Check …	
Match …	
Find …	
Complete the (dialogue).	
Listen.	
Say the words.	
Look at the picture.	
Read the (text).	
Tick …	
Add … to the (list).	
Choose (the correct answer).	
Answer the questions.	

Vocabulary

3 Look at pages 73–80 of this Workbook. Write the page numbers.

1 Map of the world   *Page 75*
2 List and translation   *page 73*
3 Word-charts   *Page 74*
4 Word-maps   *Page 74*
5 Wordlist   *Page 76*
6 Word family tree   *Page 76*
7 Picture dictionary   *Page 73*
8 Word family   *Page 76*

4 Write the words in the puzzle. Use the pictures.

Unit 1
New friends

1 Write the short forms.

1 I am a student.   *I'm a student.*

2 What is your name?   What's your name?

3 He is from England.   He's from England.

4 She is a doctor.   She's a doctor.

5 It is a hamburger.   It's a hamburger.

6 The book is from Poland.   The book's from Poland.

7 I am from Australia.   I'm from Australia.

8 My name is Kerry.   My name's Kerry.

2   a   Write introductions.

 Martina

Kate

1   *This is Martina.*   2   This is Kate.

 Leonardo

Ronaldo

3   This is Leonardo.   4   This is Ronaldo.

b   Match the people in Exercise 3a with these countries. Write sentences.

> Brazil   ~~Britain~~   ~~the USA~~   ~~Switzerland~~

1   Martina:

    She's from Switzerland.

2   Kate:

    She's from Britain

3   Leonardo:

    He's from the USA.

4   Ronaldo:

    He's from ~~Brazit~~ Brazil.

3   Find the names of the countries.

4   Write the countries under the map.

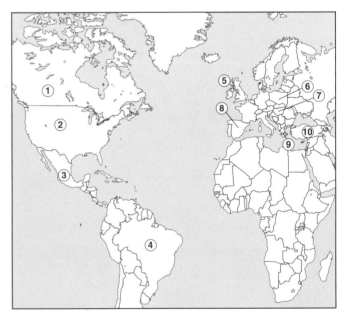

1   *Canada*   2   America   3   Mexico

4   Brazil   5   Britain   6   Poland

7   Hungary   8   Spain   9   Greece

10   Turkey

Countdown

1 Match the questions and answers.

1 What's your name? — I'm Maria.
2 Where's she from? — She's from Japan.
3 What's your phone number? — 308732.
4 Where are you from? — I'm from Italy.
5 What's your address? — 23 London Road.

2 Look at the pictures and complete the sentences with a name and *he*, *she*, *his* or *her*.

Helen

1 This is my friend. _Her_ name is **Helen** and **She** 's from Australia. **Her** phone number is 257589.

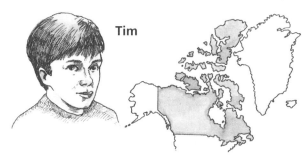

Tim

2 This is my friend, too. **His** name is **Tim** and **he** 's from Canada. **His** phone number is 581342.

Ana

3 This is another friend. **Her** name is Ana and **She** 's from Argentina. **Her** phone number is 617430.

3 Put this dialogue in the correct order.

I'm fine. How are you?   4
Hello, 64309.   1
I'm at the hotel.   6
Hi, Adam, it's Helen here.   2
Very well, thanks. Where are you?   5
Helen, hi! How are you?   3

4 Complete these lists of numbers.

1 ten, nine, eight, _seven_ , _six_ , _five_ , _four_ , _three_
2 two, four, six, _eight_ , _ten_
3 nine, seven, _five_ , _three_ , _one_
4 one, four, two, five, _three_ , _six_ , _four_ , _seven_ , _five_ , _eight_

5 Match the people with the car numbers.

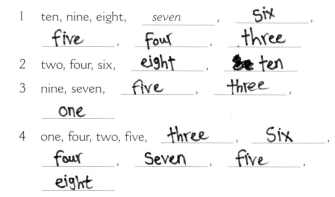

1 B 673 145   *Robert*
2 B 694 140   Louise
3 B 691 440   Paul
4 B 637 205   Janet
5 B 637 502   Michael
6 B 673 205   Lidia

What number is your car?

Paul   It's B, six, nine, one, four, four, oh.
Janet   It's B, six, three, seven, two, oh, five.
Robert   It's B, six, seven, three, one, four, five.
Lidia   It's B, six, seven, three, two, oh, five.
Michael   It's B, six, three, seven, five, oh, two.
Louise   It's B, six, nine, four, one, four, oh.

5

Pleased to meet you

1 a Say these words to yourself.

> be is meet this people please practise six

b Write the words in the correct list.

/iː/	/ɪ/
_be_	_is_
_____	_____
_____	_____
_____	_____

2 Complete the dialogue between Carol and Ricky.

Ricky Hello. My ¹ _name's_ Ricky. ² _____ your name?

Carol I'm Carol.

Ricky Pleased to ³ _____ you, Carol. ⁴ _____ from Oxford. ⁵ _____ are you from?

Carol I'm ⁶ _____ Oxford, too.

Ricky What's ⁷ _____ address?

Carol 3 Park Place, Oxford.

Ricky What's your ⁸ _____ number?

Carol It's 65189.

Ricky Here's my number.

3 Complete this dialogue about yourself.

Carol Hello. _____ name's Carol. What's _____ name?

You _____
_____ .

Carol Pleased to _____ you, _____ . I'm _____ England. _____ are you from?

You _____ from _____ .

Carol What's your address?

You _____

Carol What's your phone number?

You _____ .

Carol Here's my number.

4 a Complete these sentences.
  1 I'_ s_rr_!
  2 Ph_ne m_ l_t_r.
  3 L__k o_t!
  4 P_ea_ed to m__t y__.

b Match the sentences with the pictures.

a _____ b _____

c _____ d _____

Skills: a fax message

1 a Complete the fax message on the right. Use these words.

> brother Bye Date Dear FAX fine
> From hotel Restaurant phone number To

b Read the fax again. Match A and B.

	A			B
1	The fax		a	730 9837.
2	His fax number		b	323 7215.
3	The fax		c	to Jane Davies.
4	Her fax number	**is**	d	from Mark Thistle.
5	Mark		e	in Thames Street.
6	The restaurant		f	at a hotel in London.

1 _d_   2 __   3 __   4 __   5 __   6 __

MESSAGE — Page 1 of 1

1 _____
2 _____ : Jane Davies, 323 7215
3 _____ : Mark Thistle, 730 9837
4 _____ : 4.2.2001
5 _____ Jane

Hello! How are you? I'm ⁶_____. I'm at a ⁷_____ in London with my ⁸_____, John. Meet me later at Gino's ⁹_____ in Thames Street. Please phone me — the ¹⁰_____ of the hotel is 0171 730 9837.

¹¹_____.

Mark

---

2 Complete this fax to your friend Susanna.

- You're in New York with your brother.
- You're at Smith's Hotel.
- Ask Susanna to meet you at Dino's Restaurant later.
- Your hotel phone number is 02134 700 1689.

FAX MESSAGE — Page 1 of 1

To: Susanna Harris, 03478 651 9785

From: _____

Date: _____

_____ Susanna

Hello! How are you? I'm _____. I'm in _____ with _____. I'm at _____.

Meet me _____.

Please phone me _____.

_____.

Bye.

---

3 Put the words in the word-map.

> Brazil Britain brother eight family five
> four friend Hungary Mexico one Poland
> six Spain student ten three Turkey

Countries _____ _____
_____
_____

Unit 1

People _____ _____
_____

Numbers _____ _____
_____ _____

Prepare for Unit 2

4 Write the words in the lists. Use a dictionary.

> ant bird eighteen elephant fifteen fish
> girl man nineteen sister thirteen woman

Animals	People	Numbers
ant	_girl_	_eighteen_
_____	_____	_____
_____	_____	_____
_____	_____	_____

Unit 2

Looking around

1 **a** Complete the questions in the box with *is* or *are*.

> What _is_ this?
> Who _____ he?
> What _____ this?
> Who _____ they?
> What _____ they?
> Who _____ she?

b Write the correct questions from the box under the pictures.

1 _What is this?_ 2 _____

3 _____ 4 _____

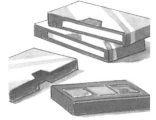

5 _____ 6 _____

c Write answers to the questions in Exercise 1b.

1 _It's a bag._
2 _____
3 _____
4 _____
5 _____
6 _____

2 Write the sentences in the plural.

1 I'm from America.
   We're from America.
2 He's in the classroom.
   They _____
3 She's in Australia.
   They _____
4 I'm at the OK Club.
   We _____
5 It's in her bag.
   They _____

3 Write the sentences with capital letters (A, B, C ...) and apostrophes (').

1 my brothers in hungary.
   My brother's in Hungary.
2 im from portugal.
   _____
3 were in this group.
   _____
4 youre a good student.
   _____
5 emma and jack are at the ok club.
   _____
6 my phone numbers 701 5763.
   _____

4 What's this? Match the pictures with the answers.

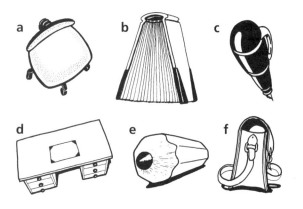

1 It's a bag. _____   4 It's a chair. _____
2 It's a pen. _____   5 It's a pencil. _____
3 It's a desk. _____   6 It's a book. _____

The Top Twenty

1 Write the questions using *this* or *that*. Then complete the short answers.

1 bird?　　*Is this a bird?*

　　　　　Yes, it is.

2 bird?　　_____

　　　　No, _____

　　　　It's Superman!

3 insect?　_____

　　　　Yes, _____

4 hamburger? _____

　　　　No, _____

　　　　It's a sandwich.

2 a Find ten words in the puzzle.

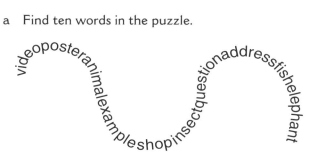

b Write the words in the chart. Remember: *an + a, e, i, o* and *u.*

a	an
video	

3 a Complete the words.

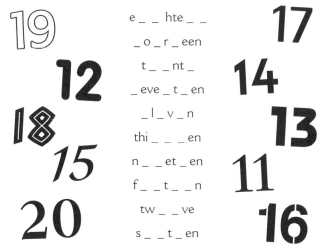

e _ _ hte _ _

_ o _ r _ een

t _ _ nt _

_ eve _ t _ en

_ l _ v _ n

thi _ _ _ en

n _ _ et _ en

f _ _ t _ _ n

tw _ _ ve

s _ _ t _ en

b Match the words and numbers.

4 a Say these words.

desk　guess　he　me　mean　pen　she
ten　three　we　well　yes

b Write the words in the correct list.

/e/	/iː/
desk	he
_____	_____
_____	_____
_____	_____
_____	_____

Help! Fire!

1 Match the sentences in A with the answers in B.

A

1 What's this in English?
2 How old are you?
3 Who's she?
4 Where are they from?
5 This is Anna.
6 What does this mean?

B

They're from Scotland.
Sorry, I don't know.
We're fourteen.
She's my sister, Anna.
It's a poster.
Pleased to meet you, Anna.

2 a Match the pictures with the correct dialogues from Exercise 1. Write the numbers in the boxes.

a ___   b ___

c ___   d _1_

e ___   f ___

b Write more dialogues from the pictures. Change some of the words.

1 Who's she? (friend)
   She's my friend.

2 This is Fran. (pleased)
   _____

3 How old are you? (15)
   _____

4 What's this in English? (picture)
   _____

5 What does this mean? (don't know)
   _____

6 Where are they from? (France)
   _____

3 Write the labels.

1 _g_
2 _s_
3 _k_
4 _f_

4 Find six animals, six people from the OK Club and two countries .

```
B V S R T Y G X W
Z N H S U R I T E
D (J A C K) I N O L
C A R O L C S F E
Z N K T Q K E I P
F E U L Q Y C S H
E M M A A N T H A
F R A N C E X T N
B I R D A V E G T
```

Animals	People	Countries
	Jack	

Skills: videos

1 **a** Read the text and write the names of the top five videos.

'Now, the top five films on video in Britain. At number five … *Three Sisters*, the new British film. *Black Shark* is at number four – but this isn't a very good film. *Friends and Family*, from American television, is at number three. This is a great film – choose this video from your video shop. *Australian Game* is at number two and, at number one again, the new film of *The Johnsons*, the American TV family. It's really very good. Now, for the top five films at the cinema …'

b Choose the correct answer.

1 *Black Shark* is about _____ .
   a a bird   **b** a fish   **c** an insect

2 *The Johnsons* and _____ are American.
   a *Three Sisters*   **b** *Black Shark*
   c *Friends and Family*

3 *The Johnsons* is about _____ .
   a animals   **b** a group of friends   **c** a family

4 _____ isn't a good video.
   a *Black Shark*   **b** *Friends and Family*
   c *Australian Game*

5 *Three Sisters* is a film from _____ .
   a America   **b** France   **c** Britain

2 **a** Put these words from Unit 2 into alphabetical order.

poster	fire	smile	kettle	boy	question

boy _____   _____   _____

_____   _____   _____

b Put these words into alphabetical order.

story	second	shop	sixteen	sister	seventeen

_____   _____   _____

_____   _____   _____

Prepare for Unit 3

3 **a** Put the animals in the correct place. Use a dictionary.

cat	dog	fish	fox	frog	giraffe	lizard
snake	spider	stick insect				

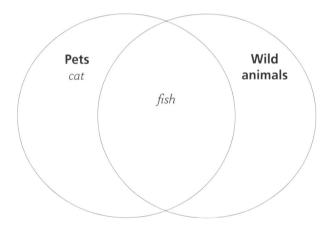

Pets
cat

fish

Wild animals

b Write the members of the family in the correct list.

brother	sister	mother	father	grandmother
grandfather				

_____   _____

_____   _____

_____   _____

Unit 3

The living world

3

1 Write about the people in the chart.

	🐱	🐕	🦎	🦜
Gina	✓	✓	✗	✗
Mark	✗	✓	✓	✗
Tim and Louise	✓	✗	✗	✓
Graham and Jill	✗	✗	✓	✓

1 Gina _has got a cat and a dog. She hasn't got a_
  lizard or a bird.

2 Mark _____

  _____

3 Tim and Louise _____

  _____

4 Graham and Jill _____

  _____

2 Write true sentences about you and your family.
Use *I've got/I haven't got* or *We've got/We haven't got* …

1 a cat

  _____

2 an aquarium

  _____

3 an English dictionary

  _____

4 a colour television

  _____

5 a big brother

  _____

6 a computer

  _____

3 Write the labels on the giraffe.

body ears eyes head leg mouth neck tail

1 _body_

2 _____

3 _____

4 _____

5 _____

6 _____

7 _____

8 _____

4 a Complete the chart.

Singular	Plural
a dog	two _dogs_
_____	four frogs
a cat	three _____
_____	two elephants
a girl	three _____
_____	twelve ants
a bird	two _____

b Write the plurals of these words ending in –*y*.

1 body   _bodies_

2 family   _____

3 secretary _____

4 country   _____

5 dictionary _____

6 university _____

Families

1 Write questions about the teenagers. Then answer the questions.

3 (eyes) *He's got big green eyes.*

You: _____

4 (nose/mouth) *He's got a small nose and mouth.*

You: _____

3 Complete a family tree for your family. Write names.

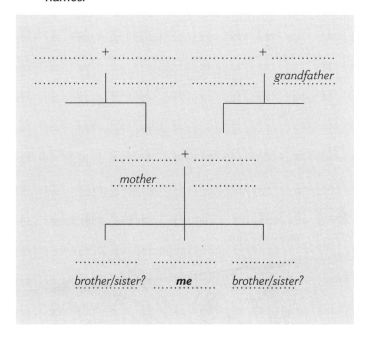

1 Jane/green eyes?

Has Jane got green eyes?

No, she hasn't. She's got blue eyes.

2 Dave/curly hair?

_____

_____

3 Ricky/fair hair?

_____

_____

4 Carol/black hair?

_____

_____

5 Emma/light brown hair?

_____

_____

2 Write sentences about your brother/sister/friend. Look at the examples to help you.

1 (old) *My brother's eleven.*

You: *My* _____

2 (hair) *He's got curly red hair.*

You: _____

4 Choose the correct word.

1 My father has got blue *eyes/ears*.
2 My grandmother is very old. She's got *black/grey* hair.
3 The tree frog has got red *eyes/legs*.
4 Our cat is *green/grey* and white.
5 The colour of cola is *red/brown*.
6 My sister has got green *hair/eyes*.

5 a Say the words in the box.

eight eye fine grey hi! my nine O<u>K</u>
say smile snake they

b Write the words in the correct list.

/eɪ/	/aɪ/
they	*fine*
_____	_____
_____	_____
_____	_____
_____	_____

What a mess!

1 Put the words in the correct order.

1 green My got eyes has mother .
My mother has got green eyes.

2 hair have straight I got .
_____

3 got hair My sister have fair and brother .
_____

4 hair tail got It long and has a curly .
_____

5 a brown moustache father got hair and My has .
_____

2 a Complete the dialogue with the sentences from the box.

> Yes, he is. Come to the club and meet him.
> It's dark brown.   He's sixteen.   No, they're blue.
> No, he hasn't.   It's short and very curly.

Debbie   Is your brother with you?

Sally   No, he isn't.

Debbie   Oh … how old is he?

Sally   ¹ _____

Debbie   What colour hair has he got?

Sally   ² _____

Debbie   Is it long or short?

Sally   ³ _____

Debbie   Has he got brown eyes, too?

Sally   ⁴ _____

Debbie   Has he got a moustache?

Sally   ⁵ _____

Debbie   Is he nice?

Sally   ⁶ _____

Debbie   Oh, OK. Good idea.

b Find Sally's brother. Tick (✓) the correct picture.

a ___

b ___

c ___

d ___

c Match these descriptions with the other three pictures.

1 He's seventeen. He's got long curly hair. He hasn't got a moustache.   _____

2 He's sixteen. He's got short brown hair. It isn't curly.   _____

3 He's seventeen. He's got short curly hair and a moustache.   _____

3 Complete the sentences with words from the box.

> pence   money   idea   sisters   ears   teacher

1 Listen! I've got a great _____ !

2 The Arctic Fox has got small _____ .

3 Oh dear. We haven't got any _____ for a hamburger.

4 Have you got any brothers or _____ ?

5 We haven't got a _____ for your class this morning.

6 Carol's only got twenty _____ .

Skills: descriptions

1 Read the description of this man and choose the correct words.

He's got *(short)*/*long fair*/*dark* hair. He's got a *big*/*small* nose and he's only got one *ear*/*eye*; it's very *small*/*big*. He's got a *big*/*small* mouth and a *long*/*short* *beard*/*moustache*.

2 Look at this picture. Write four sentences to describe the man. Use the ideas in Exercise 1 to help you.

_____

_____

_____

_____

Prepare for Unit 4

3 a Find these words in a dictionary.

> bathroom   bedroom   dining-room   kitchen
> living-room   house

b What have you got in your house? Write two things under each room.

Bathroom	**Bedroom**	**Dining-room**
_____	_____	_____
_____	_____	_____

Kitchen	**Living-room**
_____	_____
_____	_____

4 Write the English words for the clothes in the picture. Use the Wordlist for Unit 4 on page 77.

> shirt   jumper   jeans   socks   T-shirt   shoes

1 *jeans*_____   2 _____

3 _____   4 _____

5 _____   6 _____

Unit 4

4

At home

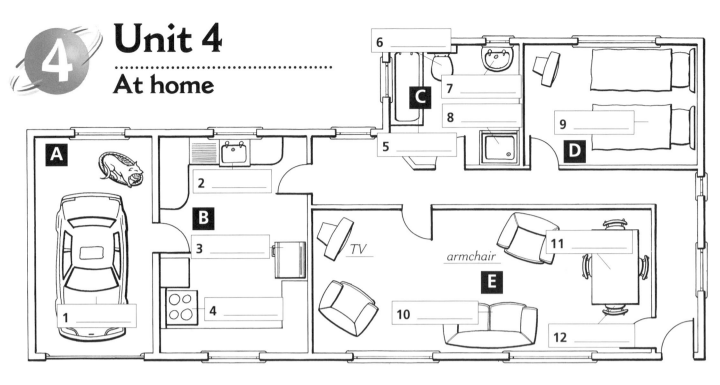

A

2 _____

B

3 _____

4 _____

1 _____

6 _____

C

7 _____

8 _____

5 _____

9 _____

D

TV

armchair

E

10 _____

11 _____

12 _____

1 a Write the labels on the rooms. Use these words.

> bathroom bedroom garage kitchen living-room

b Write the labels on the furniture. Use these words.

> basin bath bed car chair cooker fridge
> shower sink sofa table toilet

2 Complete the sentences with *There is/isn't* or *There are/aren't*, and a number if necessary.

1 *There* *is* _____ a cooker in the kitchen.

2 *There* *are* *two* _____ beds in the bedroom.

3 _____ _____ a car in the garage.

4 _____ _____ _____ armchairs in the living-room.

5 _____ _____ a dining-room in the house.

6 _____ _____ _____ chairs next to the table.

7 _____ _____ _____ bedroom in the house.

3 Answer the questions.

1 Are there two bathrooms in the house?

No, there aren't. There's one bathroom in

the house.

2 Are there three bedrooms in the house?

_____

_____

3 Are there two cars in the garage?

_____

_____

4 Are there three armchairs in the living-room?

_____

_____

5 Is there one TV in the house?

_____

_____

4 a Read this text about the house. There are three mistakes. Find the mistakes and underline them.

This house has got five rooms: a living-room, a bedroom, a kitchen and a bathroom. In the living-room there are two armchairs, a sofa, a TV, a table and six chairs next to the table. There are two beds and a TV in the bedroom. The bathroom has got a bath, a toilet and a basin but it hasn't got a shower. The kitchen has got a cooker, a sink and a fridge.

b Correct the mistakes.

1 _____

2 _____

3 _____

Shirts and skirts

1 Complete Susie's description of her room. Use *in, on, under, next to,* and *near.*

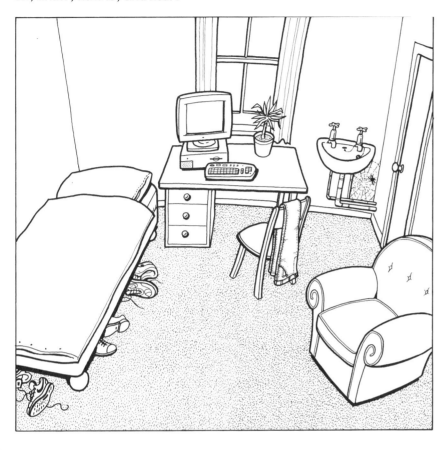

This is my bedroom. There's a bed
¹ _in_ one corner and there's a
desk ² _____ the bed. There's a
basin ³ _____ the other corner. I've
got two chairs ⁴ _____ the room:
the armchair is ⁵ _____ the door
and the other chair is ⁶ _____ the
desk. My computer is ⁷ _____
the desk, and there's a small plant
⁸ _____ it, too. I'm not very tidy:
all my shoes are ⁹ _____ the bed,
and some of my clothes are
¹⁰ _____ the chair. Oh dear, and
there's a spider ¹¹ _____ the basin!

2 Look at the pictures and write sentences.

1 *It's his shirt.*   2 _____   3 _____

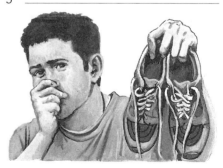

4 _____   5 _____   6 _____

3 What does the *'s* mean? Tick (✓) the correct column.

		is	*has*	Possessive
1	Andrew's from London.	✓		
2	This is Gillian's T-shirt.			✓
3	Alison's got a brother.			
4	Paul is Kate's brother.			
5	My big sister's a student.			
6	She's got an apartment in London.			
7	It's a very small apartment.			

4 Write the names of the clothes in the correct list.

helmet   jeans   jumper   shirt   shoes   skirt
socks   sweatshirt   T-shirt   trainers   trousers

Clothes for the …

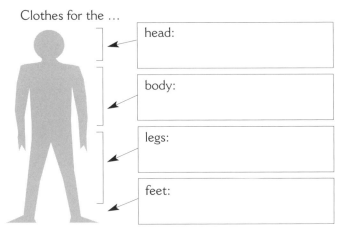

head:

body:

legs:

feet:

5 **a** Underline the correct words.

Here's Martin, with a black *jumper/shirt*, white *trousers/jeans* and black *shoes/trainers*.

b Write a description of Maria.

Here's Maria, with

_____

Emma's idea

1 What do you think of these things and people? Use the ideas in the box.

It's	amazing!
He's	fantastic!
She's	all right.
They're	not bad.
	boring!
	awful!

1 _____

_____

2 _____

_____

3 _____

_____

4 _____

_____

5 _____

_____

2 Complete the dialogues using the phrases in the box.

> This is my jumper!   See you tomorrow!
> It's not bad …   Yes, see you!   It's amazing!
> What do you think of the house?
> Your room is a real mess! Tidy it up!
> No, it's not! It's my sister's jumper!
> This is the living-room. There's a sofa and two chairs.

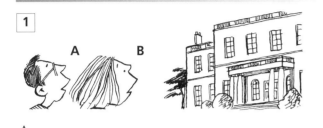

1

A _____

B _____

2

A _____

B _____

3

A _____

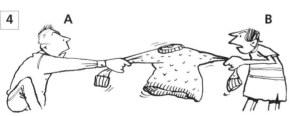

4

A _____

B _____

5

A _____

B _____

Skills: describing a room

1 a Read this text about a room. Find 16 mistakes and underline them:

6 mistakes with capital letters (A, B, C …)
4 mistakes with apostrophes (')
6 spelling mistakes

> its a big room with tow windos. ive got a large sofar under one window and there are two amchairs next to the sofa. theres a small tabel in one corner with a plant on it. theres a tv and vidio near the door.

b Write the correct text.

_____

_____

_____

_____

_____

_____

_____

Prepare for Unit 5

2 a You know some food and drink words in English. (Look at page 7 of your Student's Book.) Write them in the correct list.

Food: _____ _____

_____ _____

_____ _____

_____ _____

Drink: _____ _____

_____ _____

b Check the meaning of these words in your dictionary and write them in the lists above.

> apple   bread   chicken   lamb   lemon   milk
> potato   rice   tea   yoghurt

c From your lists, find:

two hot drinks: _____ _____

a vegetable: _____

two sorts of fruit: _____ _____

two sorts of meat: _____ _____

three cold drinks: _____ _____

_____

19

Unit 5
The best of British

1 a Change these sentences from positive to negative.

1 I like beans.

I don't like beans.

2 We eat a lot of fruit and vegetables.

_____

3 I like cheese and fruit together.

_____

4 We eat a lot of meat.

_____

b Change these sentences from negative to positive.

1 I don't like tomatoes.

_____

2 She doesn't use spicy ingredients.

_____

3 They don't enjoy cooking at home.

_____

2 Complete the dialogues with present simple verbs.

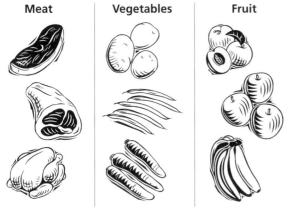

Meat	Vegetables	Fruit

1 Julia   What sort of meat ¹ _do_ you _like_ (like), Martin?

Martin   Well, I ² _____ (love) chicken and lamb, but I ³ _____ (not eat) beef.

Julia   Really? I ⁴ _____ (love) chicken, lamb and beef!

Martin   ⁵ _____ you _____ (eat) a lot of vegetables, too?

Julia   No, I ⁶ _____ . I ⁷ _____ (like) potatoes and beans, but I ⁸ _____ (not like) carrots. Do you like vegetables?

Martin   I ⁹ _____ (not like) carrots or beans, but I ¹⁰ _____ (love) potatoes.

2 Martin   Would you like some fruit, Julia? I've got apricots, apples and bananas.

Julia   Thanks. I'd like an apple. I ¹ _____ (not like) apricots or bananas.

Martin   Oh, I ² _____ (love) apricots and apples. I ³ _____ (love) bananas, too.

3 a Read the dialogues again. Complete the chart for Julia (J) and Martin (M).

J								
M								

b Write sentences about the people in the dialogues. Use *and*, *but*, and *or*.

1 Julia/beef/lamb

Julia likes beef and lamb.

2 Julia/beans/carrots

Julia likes beans but she doesn't like carrots.

3 Julia/apricots/bananas

Julia doesn't like apricots or bananas.

4 Martin/chicken/lamb

_____

_____

5 Martin/beans/carrots

_____

_____

6 Julia/apples/bananas

_____

_____

20

What would you like?

1 Write the words in the correct list.

chips money orange juice people

shoes sugar tomatoes water

Countable	Uncountable
chips	*money*
_____	_____
_____	_____
_____	_____

2 a Write the waiter's questions.

1 would / like / cheese?
Would you like any cheese?

2 would / like / ketchup / onions with your hamburger?
Would you like any ketchup or onions with
your hamburger?

3 would / like / sugar in your coffee?
_____

4 would / like / chips / beans with your pie?
_____
_____

5 would / like / ice cream?
_____

b Complete the answers to the questions.

1 No, thank you. I don't want _____ cheese.

2 I don't want _____ ketchup, but I'd like _____ onions.

3 Yes, please, and I'd like _____ milk, too.

4 Yes, please. I'd like _____ chips and _____ beans.

5 Yes, please, I'd like _____ chocolate ice cream.

3 Match the pictures and the sentences.

1 That's six pounds and twenty-five pence. _*d*_

2 Two pounds sixty, please. _____

3 They're forty-nine pounds fifty pence. _____

4 This is only ninety-six pounds and ninety-nine pence. _____

5 Eighty-five pence, please. _____

6 That's nineteen pounds ninety-eight, please. _____

4 Find twelve words for food and drink.

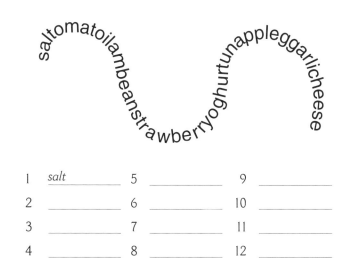

1	*salt*	5	_____	9	_____
2	_____	6	_____	10	_____
3	_____	7	_____	11	_____
4	_____	8	_____	12	_____

5 a Say these words.

buys cooks eats enjoys likes loves orders
teaches uses wants

b Write the words in the correct list.

/s/	/z/	/ɪz/
cooks	*buys*	
_____	_____	_____
_____	_____	_____
_____	_____	

Hamburgers

1 Put these words in the correct order.

1 thin   John   like   pizzas   doesn't   .
John doesn't like thin pizzas.

2 letters   your   Do   to   write   you   friends   ?

_____

3 at   English   that   Mr Smith   school   teaches   .

_____

4 sister   Does   meat   your   eat   ?

_____

5 don't   My   eggs   like   brothers   .

_____

2 The sentences in the box are from two different dialogues. Write the two dialogues.

> Can I help you?   Would you like any extras?
> Would you like any sugar with the coffee?
> Yes, I'd like a Mexican pizza, please.
> Yes, we'd like a milkshake and a coffee, please.
> OK, that's two pounds ninety, please.
> Yes, a cola, please.   Can I help you?
> Yes, please. I'd like extra cheese.
> No, thanks, but I'd like some milk.
> OK. Would you like a drink with your pizza?

1   In a pizza restaurant

Waiter   *Can I help you?* _____

Customer   _____

Waiter   _____

Customer   _____

Waiter   _____

Customer   _____

2   In a coffee bar

Waiter   *Can I help you?* _____

Customer   _____

Waiter   _____

Customer   _____

Waiter   _____

3 Write the names of these things in the lists.

Food	Drink	Clothes
_____	_____	_____
_____	_____	_____
_____	_____	_____
_____	_____	_____

4 a   Put the food and drink words from Exercise 3 in this chart.

	Food	Drink
I like		
I don't like		

b   Add two more food words and two more drink words to the chart.

c   Write two sentences about your favourite food and drink, and write two sentences about food and drink you don't like.

Example: *My favourite food is ice cream. It's delicious! I don't like eggs. They're awful.*

_____

_____

_____

_____

Skills: a menu

1 a Look at the menu. Choose one of these names for the restaurant. Write it next to 1.

Ishtar's Indian Restaurant   Pete's Pizza Palace
Peggy's Pie Place

1 _____

Today's Specials

2 _____

Lamb and apricot pie £7.50

Spicy chicken pie £5.90

Beef and mushroom pie £8.50

4 _____

Banana and chocolate £2.60

Coffee dream £2.60

Vanilla with hot chocolate sauce £2.80

3 _____

Potatoes £1.00

Beans £1.20

Salad £2.50

5 _____

Cola/Lemonade £0.90

Mineral water £0.80

Tea £0.70

Coffee/Hot chocolate £1.00

b Write these headings next to numbers 2–5.

Drinks
Meat dishes
Ice cream
Vegetables

2 Answer the questions.

1 Which dish has got meat and fruit in it?

_____

2 Which cold drinks are there on the menu?

_____

3 A customer orders spicy chicken pie with potatoes, coffee dream ice cream, and a cola. What is the price of his order?

_____

3 Continue this word-map with all the words from the menu and five other food and drink words.

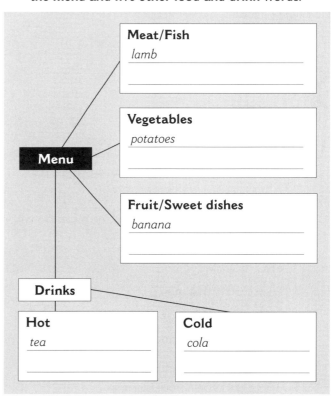

Prepare for Unit 6

4 a Find the meaning of these words. Use a dictionary.

concert sing dance musician perform
singer dancer song studio tour

b Write the words in the family tree.

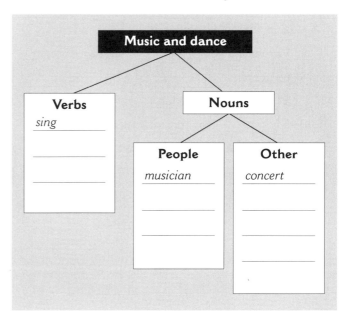

Considation

Consolidation

Check yourself
Grammar

1 Choose the correct answer.

1 My sister _____ twenty-one years old.

   a has **b** is **c** are

2 There's _____ apple on the table. Do you want it?

   a a **b** some **c** an

3 I don't know that man. _____ is he?

   a Who **b** What **c** How

4 I _____ got any money today.

   a don't have **b** hasn't **c** haven't

5 There are people from about six _____ here.

   a countrys **b** countries **c** country

6 Has your mother got _____ short hair?

   a – **b** a **c** the

7 There _____ about thirty students in this class.

   a is **b** have got **c** are

8 There's a fridge _____ the kitchen.

   a in **b** on **c** under

9 We haven't got _____ vanilla ice cream today.

   a some **b** any **c** an

10 _____ to order your meal now?

   a Would you like **b** Do you like **c** Like you

/10

2 Complete the dialogue. Use words and phrases from the box.

| do doesn't like got has got look next to that this want your |

Tony   Hi! How are you?

Louise I'm fine. Have you ¹_____ a table?

Tony   Yes. This is our table.

Louise Good. Where's ²_____ sister?

Tony   My sister? She's at home. She ³_____ this cafe.

Louise Really? I don't like some cafes, but I love ⁴_____ cafe. Do you like it?

Tony   Oh, yes, I ⁵_____! Oh, ⁶_____ at ⁷_____ apple pie! Mmm.

Louise Where?

Tony   There's a young boy ⁸_____ the window. He ⁹_____ a fantastic apple pie.

Louise Oh, yes.

Tony   Let's order. I ¹⁰_____ some of that pie!

Louise I don't. I don't like sweet things.

/10

Vocabulary

3 Underline the correct words.

1　In my family we love animals. My brother's got a large black *dog/pen* and I've got a small yellow *cat/bird*.

2　My father is very tall. He's got brown *hair/ears* and blue *hair/eyes*.

3　I've got one grandmother – my father's *sister/mother*. I've got one *grandfather/father*, too. He's my mother's father.

4　Our new house has got a big bathroom with a big *garden/bath* and a *shower/cooker*.

5　OK, stop. Close your *books/eyes* and put your *pens/chairs* on your desks.

/10

Communication

4 Match A and B to make dialogues.

A

1　Hello.
2　What's your name?
3　This is my friend Julian.
4　How are you?
5　What's this in English?
6　How old are you?
7　What's she like?
8　What do you think of it?
9　See you later!
10　Would you like a sandwich?

B

a　I'm fifteen.
b　Pleased to meet you.
c　Bye!
d　Hi!
e　No, thank you.
f　It's awful!
g　My name's Dave, Dave Hill.
h　She's got long brown hair.
i　It's a book.
j　I'm fine, thanks.

1 ___　2 ___　3 ___　4 ___　5 ___
6 ___　7 ___　8 ___　9 ___　10 ___

/10

Pronunciation

5 Say these words, then write them in the correct list. Use the sound of the underlined letters to help you.

bl<u>ue</u>　br<u>ea</u>d　fr<u>ui</u>t　gr<u>ee</u>n　l<u>a</u>st　l<u>i</u>ke　n<u>e</u>ck　sh<u>ar</u>k　t<u>ea</u>m　wh<u>i</u>te

beef /iː/	**pet** /e/	**bike** /aɪ/
_____	_____	_____
_____	_____	_____

true /uː/	**star** /ɑː/
_____	_____
_____	_____

/10

Total	/50

Review

6 Look at Units 1–5 of your Student's Book again. Add any new words to the charts on pages 73–76 of this book.

7 Do you remember the lessons from Units 1–5? Look at your scores and complete the chart for yourself.

I remember …

	60%–100% ★ ★★	40%–60% ★ ★☆	0%–40% ★ ☆☆
Grammar			
Vocabulary			
Communication			
Pronunciation			

Skills: a recipe

Reading

1 What things from the pictures do *you* usually have in a salad?

potatoes ☐   eggs ☐   onions ☐

olives ☐   carrots ☐   beans ☐

lettuce ☐   tuna ☐   tomatoes ☐

2 a Read the text about a salad from France. Are the sentences true or false? Correct the false sentences.

Cook two potatoes and some beans in water with some salt in it. Cook two eggs in hot water, too. Put some lettuce in a large bowl. Slice two tomatoes, then put the cold potatoes, beans and eggs on the lettuce in the bowl. Put the tuna and olives in the bowl too, with some olive oil, salt and pepper. Now eat your salad!

bowl

slice

1   The salad hasn't got any salt in it.
   False. The salad has got some salt in it.

2   The salad has only got vegetables in it.

3   It hasn't got any meat in it.

4   You cook all of the ingredients.

5   It hasn't got any olives in it, but it has got some olive oil in it.

b Read the text again and make a list of all the ingredients in this salad.

Writing

3 a Find ten mistakes in this letter. Underline them.

> 63 High Street
> Manchester M23 4RT
> England
>
> 6th May
>
> Dear Carol,
>
> Thank you four your letter. I'm fifteen years old. I'm tall and I've got short fair hair and blue eyes.
>
> i live in a big house in Manchester with my mother and father. I hasn't got any brothers and sisters. My fathers name is Matthew, and my mother's name is Sarah.
>
> Our house is nice. It is got four bedrooms, two bathrooms, a kichen, a living-room and a garage. My bedroom is great. There is a telephone in my room and after school I phone my friends. My father doesn't like it very much!
>
> I likes pop music and watching television. My favourite TV programme is 'The Top Twenty Show'.
>
> Well, that's all. Please write to me again.
>
> Yours,
>
> Adam

b Correct the mistakes. Write the words again.

1 _____   5 _____   8 _____

2 _____   6 _____   9 _____

3 _____   7 _____   10 _____

4 _____

Unit 6
Life and times

1 Complete the interview with the pop group *Blue Aquarium*.

a Complete the interviewer's questions with verbs from the box.

> start   travel   travel   find   visit

b Write short answers to the questions.
(✓ = *Yes, we do.* ✗ = *No, we don't.*)

1   Do you sometimes *find* time for exercise? (✓)

 Yes, we do.

2   Do you often _____ different countries? (✓)

3   Do you usually _____ by plane? (✗)

4   Do you often _____ at night? (✓)

5   Do you always _____ work in the evening? (✗)

2 Make sentences about *Blue Aquarium*. Put the words in the right order.

1   goes   usually   the   Alex   swimming   morning   in   .

 Alex usually goes swimming in the morning.

2   after   work   They   lunch   start   usually   .

3   sometimes   They   meet   on tour   friends   .

4   before   concert   never   eat   They   a   .

5   Alex   exercise   always   takes   on tour   some   .

3 Write two sentences about yourself for each picture. Use the words and phrases in the box.

> always   never   often   sometimes   usually
> in the morning   in the afternoon   in the evening
> at the weekend

Example:

I often watch TV at the weekend. I never watch TV in the morning.

1

2

3

4

4 Write the times for the clocks.

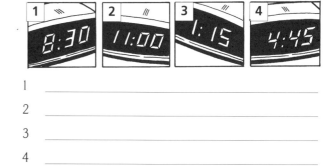

1

2

3

4

Carnival time

1 Complete this dialogue with object pronouns.

Alan Would you like to go to the carnival this week?

Lisa Good idea. When?

Alan Well, not on Saturday. Mum and Dad always visit my grandparents on Saturday, and they want ¹ _me_ to go with ² _____ this weekend.

Lisa OK … this evening, at about six o'clock?

Alan Yes. Bring your brother with ³ _____ . I like ⁴ _____ !

Lisa OK! Do you want to ask Jane?

Alan No, I don't like ⁵ _____ , and she doesn't like ⁶ _____ !

Lisa I know. Let's take our bikes with ⁷ _____ . The carnival is very big, but it's easy to see all of ⁸ _____ by bike.

Alan OK, then. See ⁹ _____ at about six.

2 Match the questions and answers.

Questions	Answers
1 Who do you meet at the weekend?	a In the morning.
2 What do people wear at carnivals?	b In the streets.
3 What do you drink in the morning?	c Colourful clothes.
4 When do you have breakfast?	d The young children.
5 Where does the carnival take place?	e My friends.
6 Who does Miss Jones teach?	f Tea.

1 _____   2 _____   3 _____
4 _____   5 _____   6 _____

3 a Write *same* or *different*.

1 colourful   black   _different_
2 exciting   boring   _____
3 huge   large   _____
4 late   last   _____
5 noisy   loud   _____

b Complete the gaps with words from Exercise 3a.

1 Come home at nine o'clock. Don't be _late_ !

2 These photographs aren't in colour. They're _____ and white.

3 Cats are small animals but giraffes are _____ animals.

4 Look at that green, blue and yellow bird. It's very _____ .

5 This story really isn't interesting. It's _____ .

6 The music at the carnival is very _____ !

4 a Say these words.

bag   cap   club   come   Dad   jumper   lamb
love   plan   salad

b Underline the /æ/ sounds in this sentence.

Dad plans to bring his black bag and jacket.

c Underline the /ʌ/ sounds in these sentences.

Hungry? Come to the club for lunch.

d Say the sentences.

The people from TV4

1 a Use the words below to complete the customer's sentences.

Customer	I / like / see some T-shirts
	I'd like to see some T-shirts.
Assistant	Certainly. What colour would you like?
Customer	I / like / green T-shirt, please
	1 _____
Assistant	I'm sorry. We haven't got any green T-shirts.
Customer	Have / got / blue T-shirts, then?
	2 _____
	_____
Assistant	Yes, we've got red, blue and yellow. Here's a blue T-shirt.
Customer	How much / it?
	3 _____
Assistant	It's six pounds.
Customer	Are / red T-shirts six pounds, too?
	4 _____
	_____
Assistant	No, they're eight pounds fifty.
Customer	OK, I / like one blue / two red T-shirts, please.
	5 _____
	_____
Assistant	Right. Here you are. That's …

b Underline the correct words.
1 The customer wants a *green/yellow* T-shirt.
2 The stall hasn't got any *blue/green* T-shirts.
3 The customer buys *two/three* T-shirts.
4 She pays *twenty pounds fifty/twenty-three pounds*.

2 Complete the dialogue. Use the information in the box.

> **Customer** You want to see some baseball caps. You'd like a red cap or a black cap. You'd also like a blue cap for your brother. How much do you pay?

Customer	1 _____
	_____
Assistant	Certainly. What colour would you like?
Customer	2 _____
	_____
Assistant	I'm sorry. We haven't got any red caps.
Customer	3 _____
	_____
Assistant	Yes, we've got black, blue and white. Here's a black cap.
Customer	4 _____
	_____
Assistant	It's three pounds fifty.
Customer	5 _____
	_____
Assistant	No, they're four pounds.
Customer	6 _____
	_____
Assistant	Right. Here you are. That's …

3 Match a verb from A with a word or phrase from B.

A		B	
1	take	a	the guitar
2	take	b	place
3	play	c	exercise
4	play	d	a TV programme
5	listen to	e	a costume
6	watch	f	volleyball
7	wear	g	music

1 _____   2 _____   3 _____   4 _____
5 _____   6 _____   7 _____

Skills: timetables

1 Read the text about Thomas. Complete his timetable.

'My day starts at eight o'clock when I have breakfast. I leave home for school at half-past eight. I always walk to school. School starts at ten to nine. We stop for lunch at twenty past twelve. I usually go home but I sometimes eat at school. I leave school at quarter to four and I usually go to the park with my friends and we play football. I go home at quarter past five and do my homework. We have supper at half past six then I watch TV or listen to music. I go to bed at ten o'clock.'

8.00	_He has breakfast._
8.30	
8.50	
12.20	
3.45	
5.15	
6.30	
10.00	

2 a Answer these questions about **your** day. Write the times.

1 What time do you have breakfast? _____

2 What time do you leave home for school? _____

3 What time does school start? _____

4 What time do you have lunch? _____

5 What time do you leave school? _____

6 What time do you arrive at home? _____

7 What time do you have supper? _____

8 What time do you go to bed? _____

b Complete this text about your day.

My day starts at _____
when I have _____. I leave home at
_____. I always
_____. School starts at
_____ and we stop for
lunch at _____. I usually
_____ for lunch. I leave
school at _____ in the
afternoon and then I _____.
We have supper at _____
and in the evening I often _____.
I go to bed at _____.

Prepare for Unit 7

3 a Look at the pictures and the sentences.

1 There are two circles and two triangles in this bicycle.

2 There are five squares, a rectangle and a triangle in this house.

Now match the words in the box with the shapes below.

circle ☐	rectangle ☐	square ☐	triangle ☐

| a | b | c | d |

b Complete these descriptions with words from the box. Use a dictionary.

Earth	space	space station	Sun

1 _____ = the world; where we all live

2 _____ = a large workplace in space

3 _____ = this is outside the Earth

4 _____ = the Earth goes around this

Unit 7
Imagine this ...

1 Jeff's room is in a mess. Complete the dialogue with *this*, *that*, *these* and *those*.

Mum Jeff, look at your room. What a mess! Come on, let's tidy it.

Jeff OK, Mum. Well, the desk is OK …

Mum No, it isn't! Where do all ¹ *those* discs go?

Jeff ² _____ discs? I want them here, near the computer.

Mum OK, put ³ _____ pencils and envelopes away, then.

Jeff OK. I don't want the envelopes, but I want ⁴ _____ pencils on the desk, and ⁵ _____ dictionary …

Mum Yes, ⁶ _____ dictionary is from the living-room. Give it to me. And why is ⁷ _____ ball in your room and not in the garden?

Jeff Um … I don't know …

2 a Match the things in A with the actions in B.

A	B
1 A CD player	check new words
2 A dictionary	write notes and answers in
3 A bag	play compact discs
4 A notebook	brush your hair
5 A hairbrush	carry things

b Write a sentence about each of the things in A.

1 *It's for playing compact discs.* _____

2 _____

3 _____

4 _____

5 _____

3 a Write the names of the shapes.

a side

1 It has got three sides. _____

2 It has got four sides. Two are long and two are short. _____

3 It hasn't got any sides. _____

4 Its four sides are all the same. _____

b Look at the picture. Write the names of the things in the correct column.

Circular	Rectangular	Square	Triangular
_____	_____	_____	_____
_____	_____	_____	_____

Clever inventions

1 a Match the parts of words. Write the complete words next to the pictures.

A
| bot | bre | cof | enve |
| mat | pai | str | whe |

B
| ad | ches | el | fee |
| ing | lope | nt | tle |

paint

_____   _____   _____   _____

b Write the words from Exercise 1a in the correct column.

Countable	**Uncountable**
bottle	_____
_____	_____
_____	_____
_____	_____

2 Complete the sentences about each picture. Use _is/are_ and _a little_, _a few_ or _a lot of_.

1 There _____ _____ matches in the box.

2 There _____ _____ water in the glass.

3 There _____ _____ bottles on the table.

4 There _____ _____ coffee in the jar.

5 There _____ _____ paint on the wall.

6 There _____ _____ tins of paint on the table.

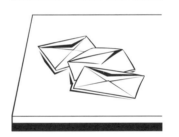

7 There _____ _____ envelopes on the desk.

3 Write sentences about yourself. Use _a lot of_, _a little_, _a few_ or _don't … any_.

1 eat/sweets

_____

_____

2 drink/milk

_____

_____

3 do/homework

_____

_____

4 take/sugar in tea and coffee

_____

_____

5 take/exercise

_____

_____

4 Complete the dialogue using the phrases in the box.

> a few   a lot of them   a little   Have you got any
> How much is that   I'd like a little   I'd like some
> only a few

In a food shop

Assistant   Hello, Mr Lewis. How are you today?

Mr Lewis   Fine thank you. ¹ *Have you got any*
            red apples today?

Assistant   Yes, here. Would you like some?

Mr Lewis   Yes, please, but ² _____.
            I'd like four, please. Can you cut
            ³ _____ Swiss
            cheese for me too, please?

Assistant   Certainly. Is that OK?

Mr Lewis   Yes, fine. ⁴ _____
            olives, too, please – those small olives.

Assistant   Just ⁵ _____ of
            those?

Mr Lewis   No, I'd like quite ⁶ _____,
            please. And ⁷ _____
            rice, just a small bag, please.

Assistant   Is that all?

Mr Lewis   Yes. ⁸ _____?

Assistant   It's three pounds and sixty pence, please.

5 Look at the invention and match the questions and answers.

Questions	Answers
1 What's it for?	It's quite big.
2 What shape is it?	No, it doesn't.
3 What size is it?	It's for washing a car.
4 Does it move? How?	It's round.
5 Does it use electricity?	Yes, it does. It's got wheels.

Project OK

1 Complete the gaps with *this*, *that*, *these* or *those*.

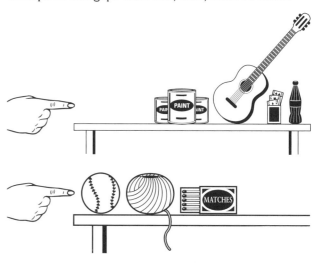

1 I'd like *that* bottle, please.
2 I'd like _____ matches, please.
3 I'd like _____ string, please.
4 I'd like _____ cards, please.
5 I'd like _____ tins, please.
6 I'd like _____ ball, please.
7 I'd like _____ guitar, please.

2 a Match the sentences in A with the replies in B to make five mini-dialogues.

	A	B
1	We've got £100!	Yes, please.
2	What about grey walls?	White? That's a good idea.
3	Would you like lunch now?	No way! Grey is boring!
4	Let's paint the walls white!	Never mind. The other shop is open.
5	Oh no! It's closed.	Good! That's a lot!

b Match the situations with the dialogues in Exercise 2a.

	Situation	Dialogue
a	Two people are shopping. It's one o'clock and they want to eat.	_____
b	Two people are shopping in the evening. It's late.	_____
c	Two people want some money to buy things for their home.	_____
d	Two people want to paint their home in different colours. (two dialogues)	_____

Skills: puzzles

1 Match these puzzles with the pictures. Write the letter (A–D) and name of the object. (Be careful – there are three puzzles and four objects!)

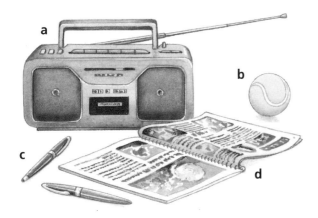

1 It's paper. It's rectangular. You use it for reading about your favourite pop stars and film stars.

_____

2 They're long and thin, and they're not very large. You use them for writing things in your notebook.

_____

3 It's round and it's small. It's usually yellow. We use it when we play tennis.

_____

2 a The puzzles match with three pictures. What is the object in the other picture?

_____

b Describe the object.

_____

_____

_____

3 Find words from the box which rhyme with the underlined word in each sentence.

| meat | men | shoes | toy | wood | plan |

1 Dan's the <u>man</u> with a _plan_ .

2 It's <u>good</u> that it's _____ .

3 I want to <u>eat</u> some _____ .

4 Don't <u>lose</u> your _____ .

5 Give the <u>boy</u> a _____ .

6 The <u>ten</u> _____ are here.

Prepare for Unit 8

4 a Read the text and write the days of the week in the diary.

Friday   Monday   Saturday   Thursday
Wednesday   Sunday   Tuesday

Monday	swimming
_____	guitar lesson
_____	homework
_____	swimming
_____	dance class
_____	tennis
_____	grandparents – lunch

I'm always very busy. On Mondays and Thursdays I go swimming after school. On Tuesdays I have a guitar lesson after school and on Fridays I have a dance class. On Wednesdays I usually go home after school and do my homework all evening. On Saturdays I play tennis with my friends in the morning and I often go to the cinema in the afternoon. On Sundays we all visit my grandparents for lunch.

b Look at these sports and activities. Write them in the word-map – use a dictionary to help you. You can use some of the words twice.

aerobics   badminton   basketball   football
judo   riding a bicycle   swimming   volleyball
walking   water aerobics

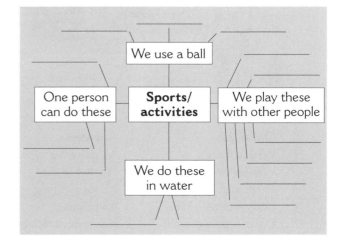

Unit 8
That's amazing

1 Look at the chart. Write short answers to these questions.

	🏇	🚶20km	🏃	🥁	🏊
Eleni	✓	✓	✓	✗	✗
Levent	✓	✗	✓	✗	✓
Magda	✓	✗	✓	✓	✗
Carlos	✗	✓	✗	✓	✓

1 Can Magda ride a horse? *Yes, she can.*

2 Can Carlos run fast? *No, he can't.*

3 Can Eleni play the drums? (she)

4 Can Levent swim? (he)

5 Can Eleni walk for 20 kilometres?

6 Can Carlos ride a horse?

7 Can Magda and Levent run fast?

2 Write sentences about the people in the chart. Use *and*, *but* or *or* to join them.

1 Eleni/ride a horse/run fast
Eleni can ride a horse and run fast.

2 Levent/ride a horse/play the drums
Levent can ride a horse but he can't play the drums.

3 Magda/swim/walk for 20 kilometres
Magda can't swim or walk for 20 kilometres.

4 Carlos/walk for 20 kilometres/run fast

5 Eleni/play the drums/swim

6 Levent/swim/run fast

3 a Match four of these activities with the pictures.

riding a bike ☐   riding a horse ☐
playing football ☐   playing volleyball ☐
cooking ☐   speaking English ☐

b What can the people in the pictures do? What can't they do? Write a sentence about each person.

1 _____

2 _____

3 _____

4 _____

4 Give **your** opinion. Use the phrases from the box.

I agree.   I think that's right.
No, I don't think so.   I'm not sure about that.

1 English is an easy language.

2 Football is a boring sport.

3 Cats are beautiful animals.

4 American pop music is awful.

Do you want to be a champion?

1 Make sentences with *must* about these sports club rules.

Sports Club | **rules**

1 Wear the correct sports clothes for your sport.

2 Wear trainers in the gym.

3 Pay for aerobics classes before they start.

4 Use the correct equipment.

5 Put the equipment away after games or classes.

1 *We must wear the correct sports clothes for our sport.*

2 _____

3 _____

4 _____

5 _____

2 a Complete the phrases. Write *in*, *at* or *on*.

1 _____ the morning

2 _____ Wednesday

3 _____ Saturday evening

4 _____ three o'clock

5 _____ winter

6 _____ the weekend

7 _____ the afternoon

8 _____ night

9 _____ Sunday night

10 _____ half past two

b Write sentences about these signs and notices. Use *in*, *at* or *on*.

1 JIM'S GYM
Open Saturday
7.30 a.m.

2 *English class*
Tuesday 4.00 p.m.

3 **Club closed**
11 p.m.

4 *Swimming pool*
Summer closing time
6.15 p.m

1 *Jim's gym opens at half past seven on Saturday morning.*

2 _____

3 _____

4 _____

3 Work out the days and complete the dates.

1 *Monday*   1st June

2 *Tuesday*   2nd June

3 _____ 8th June

4 _____ 10th June

5 _____ 13th June

6 _____ 18th June

7 _____ 19th June

8 _____ 21st June

4 a Write the names of the sports.

1 loblatfo   *football*

2 douj   _____

3 nurning   _____

4 simwingm   _____

5 dabnitmon   _____

6 oarescib   _____

7 lblalelvoy   _____

8 lblasabtek   _____

36

b Answer the questions with the sports from Exercise 4a.

1 Which sports do you usually play in a gym?
aerobics, basketball, badminton, judo

2 Which sports do you usually play in summer?

3 Which sports can you play with only one other person?

4 Which sports do **you** like?

5 Rewrite this text with the correct punctuation. Find:

3 mistakes with full stops (.)
7 mistakes with capital letters (A, B, C …)
8 mistakes with apostrophes (')

my friends gym is open every day of the week its open from seven oclock in the morning until eleven oclock at night from monday to friday on saturday its open from eight in the morning to eleven at night and on sunday its open from nine oclock in the morning to ten oclock at night

Where's the money?

1 Read the phone conversation and put the phrases from the box in the correct place.

Hang on a minute.	How are you?
Monday evening	That's not good enough!
in the morning	What time?

Emily Hello Laura, it's Emily here.

Laura Hi, Emily. ¹_____

Emily I'm fine. Listen, Laura. I'm sorry, but I can't play badminton with you on ²_____ .

Laura Oh, Emily! ³_____
We can't play on Monday with only three people!

Emily I know. Can we play another day?

Laura I don't know. ⁴_____
Here's my diary. When do you want to play?

Emily Wednesday evening?

Laura OK … oh, no, I can't play on Wednesday evening. I've got a guitar lesson at seven. What about Thursday evening?

Emily Yes, I can play on Thursday. ⁵_____

Laura Half past seven?

Emily OK. What about the others? Can you tell them?

Laura Yes, I can do that before school starts
⁶_____ .

Emily OK. Thanks, Laura. Bye.

Laura Bye.

Skills: sports routines

1 Read this text about Russell, an athlete, and correct the sentences about him.

'I love sport. I play basketball for my city and I train for a few hours every day. Of course, I work too, but only in the mornings. On Mondays to Fridays I start my day at the swimming pool. I swim from seven o'clock to eight o'clock every day. Then I go to work. I finish work at one o'clock and then I train in the gym for an hour on Mondays, Tuesdays and Fridays. On Wednesdays and Thursdays I go running. I have lunch at about two o'clock. Then I watch training videos and videos of our last games. The team meets at six every evening from Monday to Thursday for an hour's basketball training. Then we play a game.

Saturdays and Sundays are different. On Saturdays we train in the gym in the morning and then we usually play a match in the afternoon. We're usually free on Sundays, but it's a hard timetable!'

1 Russell doesn't like sport.
He loves sport.

2 He can't play basketball.

_____

3 He trains for an hour every day.

_____

4 He starts his day at the track.

_____

5 He doesn't have time to do any work.

_____

6 He never goes running.

_____

7 He usually plays a basketball match on Sundays.

_____

2 Complete Russell's timetable. Use these words.

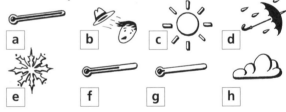

basketball training   free   have lunch   play a game
play a match   run   swim   train in the gym
watch videos   work

	Mon	Tues	Wed	Thur	Fri	Sat	Sun
7.00-8.00	←		*swim*		→		↑
9.00-1.00							
1.00-2.00							
2.00-3.00							*free*
3.00-5.30							
6.00-7.00							
7.00-8.00							↓

Prepare for Unit 9

3 a Match these words with the pictures. Use a dictionary.

a	b	c	d
e	f	g	h

1 cloud _____   5 snow _____

2 cold _____   6 sun _____

3 hot _____   7 warm _____

4 rain _____   8 wind _____

b Match these phrases with the pictures in Exercise 3a.

1 It's sunny. _____

2 It's windy. _____

3 It's cloudy. _____

4 It's wet. _____

9 Unit 9
Travelling

1 Look at the pictures and then complete the sentences using the verbs in the box.

arriving carrying changing diving leaving
looking relaxing riding running smiling
sleeping swimming

1 Kevin *is arriving* and he *'s looking* for his friend.

2 He _____ some money. He _____ a big bag.

3 He _____ for a bus. The bus _____ .

4 He _____ a bike. He _____ .

5 He _____ and scuba _____ in the sea.

6 He _____ on a beach. He _____ .

2 Make questions about the pictures in Exercise 1.

1 arrive/at a station?
Is Kevin arriving at a station?

2 change/his money?
_____

3 run/for a taxi?
_____

4 ride/a horse?
_____

5 swim/in a lake?
_____

6 sleep/on the beach?
_____

3 Put the verbs from Exercise 1 into three groups. Look at the spelling.

+ *ing*	− *e* + *ing*	+ consonant + *ing*
carrying	*arriving*	*running*

4 a Find six words for places.

1 refe *reef*   4 tianmonu _____
2 esa _____   5 sildan _____
3 echab _____   6 stoca _____

b These two words are from other units. Can you remember them?

7 ekal _____   8 stefor _____

c Underline the correct words.

Australia is a very large ¹*sea/island* with a lot of interesting plants and animals. There is a beautiful, huge ²*coral reef/forest* in eastern Australia, along the ³*mountain/coast*, but there are problems because tourists are breaking it. Also in eastern Australia there are some large ⁴*mountains/beaches*, called the Australian Alps. People go skiing there in the winter. Australia has got some very nice ⁵*forests/beaches* and people come to these in the summer to go swimming in the ⁶*sea/lakes*.

Having a wonderful time … ?

1 Complete the lists with adjectives or adverbs.

	Adjective	Adverb
1	bad	_____
2	careful	_____
3	hungry	_____
4	_____	loudly
5	miserable	_____
6	quiet	_____
7	_____	steadily
8	_____	well
9	hard	_____
10	fast	_____

2 Describe these pictures. Use a verb from the box and an adverb from Exercise 1.

dance	run	speak	walk

1   *He's speaking loudly.*

2   _____

3   _____

4   _____

3 Write sentences about the weather.

1 *It's hot.*   2 _____ 3 _____ 4 _____

5 _____   6 _____   7 _____   8 _____

4 a Read about the weather in England and Wales. Draw the correct symbols in the boxes on the map.

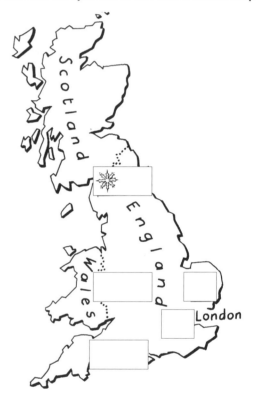

In the north of England and Scotland it's snowing today and it's very cold – only five degrees. In the west of England and Wales it's raining but it's warm (20 degrees). In the east it's very windy and in London it's cloudy. In the south it's sunny and hot (28 degrees).

b Write a short weather report about your country at this time of the year.

_____

_____

_____

_____

Detective work

1 Describe each person in the picture. Use verbs and adverbs from the box.

Verbs: carry play run sit talk talk
Adverbs: angrily badly carefully loudly
miserably quickly

1 The old woman *is talking angrily.* _____

2 The young man _____

3 The two women _____

4 The boy _____

5 The waiter _____

6 The two girls _____

2 Complete the phone call. Use the sentences from the box.

> What's the weather like?   I'm going now, Mum.
> I'm watching football on TV.
> The sun's shining and it's warm.
> Are you enjoying the camp?   I'm fine, thanks.

Chris   Hello, Mum.

Mum   Oh, hello, Chris. How are you?

Chris   ¹ _____

Mum   Oh, good. ² _____

_____

Chris   Yes, I am. It's great here!

Mum   ³ _____

Chris   It's beautiful! ⁴ _____

_____

Mum   That's nice. What are you doing now?

Chris   ⁵ _____ It's a

great game! ⁶ _____

Mum   OK, then. Enjoy the next few days.

Chris   Thanks. Bye.

3 Underline the odd one out in each group.

1 cloudy   windy   busy   sunny
2 quickly   nationality   immediately   miserably
3 snowing   laughing   diving   sing
4 airport   coral reef   mountain   forest
5 traveller   tourist   passenger   police officer
6 local   hard   fast   well
7 rain   pollution   snow   sun
8 fisherman   police officer   package holiday
   tour guide

Skills: postcards

1 a Circle the correct words in the postcard.

b What do these underlined pronouns refer to?

1 'you' in line 1 _____

2 'It' in line 2 _____

3 'it' in line 4 _____

4 'They' in line 6 _____

5 'it' in line 7 _____

6 'we' in line 8 _____

Dear Maria,
How are <u>you</u>? We're having a ¹**great/** (**terrible**) time here! The weather is ²**fantastic/awful**. <u>It</u>'s really cold and ³**wet/noisy**. The hotel is very ⁴**interesting/uncomfortable** and <u>it</u>'s ⁵ **boring/noisy**. We ⁶**don't like/wouldn't like** the people here. <u>They</u>'re ⁷**friendly/miserable**. And we don't eat the food because <u>it</u>'s really ⁸**delicious/terrible**. At the moment <u>we</u> are ⁹**sitting in the sun/sitting in our room** near the window and we are ¹⁰**watching the rain/playing volleyball**.

See you soon.

Alex and Susan

2 Complete a similar postcard. This time, write about a good holiday.

Dear _____

How are you? We're having _____

_____.

The weather is _____. The hotel is _____. The people are _____ and the food is _____. At the moment we're _____ and we're _____.

See you soon.

_____

Prepare for Unit 10

3 Read the clues and write the names of the months in the calendar.

Clues

1 December is the last month of the year.

2 July and August come together – they are the main months of the European summer.

3 April is the month after March.

4 February is the second month.

5 October comes after September and November comes before December.

6 May is a lovely month. It comes before June.

January		March		June
1	1	1	1	1
2	2	2	2	2
3	3	3	3	3
4	4	4	4	4
5	5	5	5	5
6	6	6	6	6
7	7	7	7	7

	September			
1	1	1	1	1
2	2	2	2	2
3	3	3	3	3
4	4	4	4	4
5	5	5	5	5
6	6	6	6	6
7	7	7	7	7

Unit 10
Diet and lifestyle

1 Lucy is visiting her grandparents in France this
week. Look at the pictures. Complete the
sentences about what she usually does and what
she's doing this week.

1. Lucy usually _gets up_ at seven o'clock but this
   week she _is staying_ in bed.
2. Lucy usually _____ to school but this week
   she _____ to the beach.
3. She usually _____ French but this week she
   _____ French.
4. She usually _____ warm clothes but this
   week she _____ a skirt and a t-shirt.
5. She usually _____ TV in the evening but
   this week she _____ with friends.
6. She usually _____ to bed at 9.30 but this
   week she _____ to bed at 11.00.

2 Complete this phone conversation between Lucy
and a friend, Steve.

Steve   Hi, Lucy. What are you doing at the moment?

Lucy   have/breakfast
I'm having breakfast.

Steve   usually/have breakfast/10.30?
Do you usually have breakfast at half past ten?

Lucy   no/usually/have breakfast/8.00

_____

_____

Steve   what/eat?

_____

Lucy   eat/fruit and yoghurt

_____

Steve   usually/have/fruit and yoghurt/breakfast?

_____

_____

Lucy   no/usually/have/an egg

_____

Steve   what/drink/with breakfast today?

_____

_____

Lucy   drink/fresh orange juice

_____

Steve   Lucky you!

43

3 Write these words as numbers.

1 a hundred and ten _____

2 two hundred and thirty-seven _____

3 four thousand, seven hundred
and ninety-two _____

4 sixteen thousand, one hundred
and thirty-one _____

5 ninety-six thousand, five
hundred and two _____

6 seven hundred and twenty-eight
thousand, four hundred and
eighty-seven _____

Pocket money

1 Write questions about the things in the picture.
Use *How much* or *How many*.

1 biscuits   2 water

3 sugar   4 passport

5 sweets   6 ice cream

7 money   8 cakes

1   *How many biscuits are there?*

2 _____

3 _____

4 _____

5 _____

6 _____

7 _____

8 _____

2 Match the words and the numbers.

1	fifteenth	a	⅓
2	a quarter	b	62%
3	a third	c	£2.20
4	ninety-nine per cent	d	31st
5	two pounds twenty	e	¼
6	thirty-first	f	15th
7	sixty-two per cent	g	£10.50
8	ten pounds fifty	h	99%

1 _____   2 _____   3 _____   4 _____

5 _____   6 _____   7 _____   8 _____

3 a   Write the dates in circles.

1   *12th January*   5 _____

2 _____   6 _____

3 _____   7 _____

4 _____

b   Choose three important dates in your country.
Why are they important?

Example: *1st January – it's New Year's Day.*

1 _____

2 _____

3 _____

The trick

1 Put the verbs in brackets '( )' in the correct tense. Use the present simple or continuous.

Presenter   What ¹ _do_ you usually _do_ (do) at the club?

Emma   We usually ² _____ (play) cards or ³ _____ (listen) to music. But this evening we ⁴ _____ (watch) a video.

Sally   ⁵ _____ you _____ (stay) in a hotel at the moment?

Mike   Yes, but we usually ⁶ _____ (stay) with friends when we ⁷ _____ (come) here.

Andy   What ⁸ _____ Geri _____ (do) at the moment?

Lisa   She ⁹ _____ (train) for the volleyball team at the moment.
She ¹⁰ _____ (play) volleyball every Saturday.

2 Answer the questions about yourself. Use the correct tense.

1   What time is it? _____

2   What do you usually do at this time? _____
_____

3   What are you doing now? _____
_____

4   When do you usually study English? _____
_____

5   What are you learning at the moment? _____
_____

6   What are your parents doing now? _____
_____

3 Dave and Carol are in a shop. Complete the dialogue with words from the box.

> birthday   brilliant   expensive   fifteen pounds
> find out   how much   See you   silly
> We'd like   What about

Dave   Look, Carol. This is a nice picture. Let's buy it as a ¹ _____ present for Dad.

Carol   That's a ² _____ idea, Dave. Let's ³ _____ the price. Excuse me, ⁴ _____ is this picture?

Assistant   It's ⁵ _____.

Dave   Oh, that's ⁶ _____, Carol.

Carol   Don't be ⁷ _____, Dave. You've got £5.00 and I've got £5.00. ⁸ _____ Mum? She can give us £5.00 too.

Dave   Oh, yes, you're right. OK. ⁹ _____ that picture, please.

Carol   Dave, the birthday cards are over there. I'd like to choose a card for Dad. ¹⁰ _____ in a minute.

Dave   OK. Fine.

4 When can you use these phrases? Match each phrase with a situation.

> That's brilliant!   What about Jack?
> See you in a minute.   Six is fine.   That's silly.

1   Your friend wants to meet you this evening at six o'clock. _____

2   Your friend has a very good idea. _____
_____

3   Your friend has a bad idea. _____

4   Your friend wants to look at another part of the shop. _____

5   Your friend thinks you must tell Jack.
_____

Skills: diagrams

1 a Jack is talking about how he spends his pocket money. How much does he spend on:

    1   coffee and biscuits?   *£1.00*

    2   presents and clothes?   _____

    3   magazines and cassettes?   _____

    4   swimming?   _____

    5   going out with friends?   _____

    6   sweets?   _____

'My pocket money? Mmm, I get twelve pounds a week. I put about a third of it away in the bank for presents and clothes. Then I spend another quarter of it on magazines and cassettes. I spend about two pounds on going out with my friends – we go out about once a week – and one pound fifty on going swimming – I go swimming on Thursdays. I spend about a pound a week at the club on coffee and biscuits, and then I spend the other fifty pence on sweets. I think that's it.'

b Use the text and your answers to Exercise 1a to complete this pie chart. Write amounts of money and items on the lines.

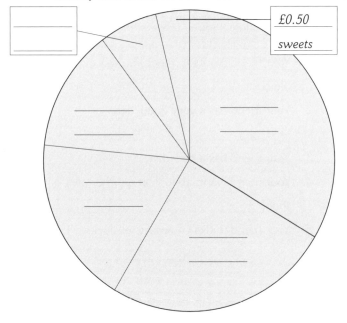

2 Look at this pie chart. Write a paragraph about Carol's spending.

Carol's pocket money: £10.00 a week

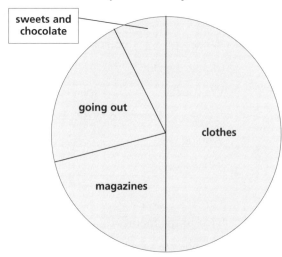

'My pocket money is ten pounds a week. I spend

_____

_____

_____

_____

_____

_____

_____

_____ ,

Prepare for Unit 11

3 Check the meanings of these words and put them in the correct list. Use a dictionary.

> damaged lovely safe terrifying violent
> survival alive frightening

Positive meaning   Negative meaning

lovely   *damaged*

_____   _____

_____   _____

_____

Considation

Check yourself
Grammar

1 Choose the correct answer.

1 Gina doesn't like ice cream. She _____ eats it.

 a always **b** never **c** often

2 Don't ask Maria to come – she _____ late.

 a always is **b** always **c** is always

3 That's my bag! Give it to _____!

 a me **b** I **c** my

4 'Can I have some of your cola?'

 'Yes, but I've only got _____ – don't drink it all!'

 a a few **b** a lot **c** a little

5 Dave is amazing – he _____ speak five languages really well!

 a can't **b** can **c** must

6 I'm learning to play the piano. I _____ practise for an hour every day.

 a must **b** can **c** can't

7 Can you see Kevin? Yes, he _____ next to the pool.

 a sits **b** sitting **c** is sitting

8 You're talking very _____. I can't hear you.

 a loudly **b** quietly **c** quiet

9 _____ rice have we got?

 a How **b** How many **c** How much

10 We _____ our friends in the city every month.

 a visit **b** are visiting **c** visiting

/10

2 Complete the dialogue. Use words and phrases from the box.

| at | can | come | me | much | o'clock |
| on | past | standing | well | | |

Guide Good morning. My name's Angela and I'm your guide for the week. This morning I want to introduce you to the hotel and the town. First, the hotel. All the waiters and the other people in the hotel [1]_____ speak English very [2]_____ – don't worry about the language! They can help you with any problems. Also, I [3]_____ to the hotel [4]_____ Tuesday and Thursday mornings [5]_____ half [6]_____ ten. You can talk to [7]_____ then, but I leave at twelve [8]_____ on those days. Now, we have different tours every day to interesting places, and I can tell you about …

Tourist How [9]_____ are they?

Guide They're different prices. Carlos can tell you the prices later. He's [10]_____ over there, by the swimming pool. Hi, Carlos!

/10

Vocabulary

3 a Underline the 'odd one out' in these lists of words.

1 Monday <u>Chinese</u> Wednesday Saturday
2 circle square triangle hot
3 volleyball mountain beach coast
4 March August February Friday
5 tennis rectangle football judo
6 sunny lake windy cold

b Complete these sentences with the 'odd ones out' from Exercise 3a.

1 _____ is a good day because we always have sport in the afternoon at school.

2 I love the summer because the weather is

    _____ .

3 It's an interesting shape – it's a _____ with a triangle in it.

4 We sometimes swim in the _____ near our house.

5 Would you like to play _____ with us?

/10

Communication

4 Match A and B.

A
1 When do you usually play football?
2 What time is it?
3 What shape is it?
4 What's it for?
5 How much cola have we got?
6 Can you ride a horse?
7 What's the weather like?
8 Can she sing well?
9 Can I use your phone?
10 When's your birthday?

B
a It's hot and sunny.
b Yes, sure.
c It's for sending messages.
d In the afternoons.
e Yes, she can sing beautifully.
f It's on 10th October.
g It's circular.
h We've only got a little.
i It's quarter to three.
j No, I can't.

1 ____ 2 ____ 3 ____ 4 ____ 5 ____
6 ____ 7 ____ 8 ____ 9 ____ 10 ____

/10

Pronunciation

5 a Which word in each list has the same sound as the example word? Underline it.

1 <u>th</u>ese: sister thing that birthday
2 si<u>ng</u>: kitchen amazing into hand
3 can't: must can money start
4 four<u>th</u>: watch this seventh tree
5 thous<u>and</u>: bank day pound the

b Put these words in the correct list.

bank drum fat junk stand sun

man /æ/   must /ʌ/
bank _____   _____

_____   _____

_____   _____

/10

Total	**/50**

Review

6 Look at Units 6–10 of your Student's Book again. Add any new words to the charts on pages 73–76 of this book.

7 Do you remember the lessons from Units 6–10? Look at your scores and complete the chart for yourself.

I remember …

	60%–100% ★ ★★	40%–60% ★ ★☆	0%–40% ★ ☆☆
Grammar			
Vocabulary			
Communication			
Pronunciation			

Skills: surveys

Reading

1 a Read the survey. Is it about:
1. sports?
2. languages?
3. homework?

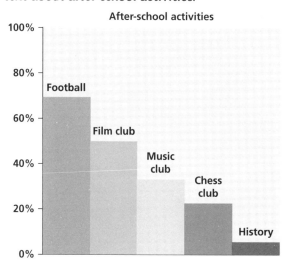

In my school there are 1,000 students. We're really lucky because we can study a lot of different languages – five! Schools in England don't usually offer five languages. They usually offer only two or three. Of course, a lot of students study French – about 65 per cent. It's very popular because it's a useful language. A lot of us go to France on holiday. Spanish is quite popular too – about 40 per cent of us study Spanish. One of the teachers gives German classes, but it's not a very popular language. Only about ten per cent of us study it – usually the boys. We have a lot of students from India in our school and they can study Hindi – an Indian language. About 20 per cent of our students learn Hindi. The other language is new to our school – it's Russian. A few students are taking it this year – about 25 per cent. I love languages. I'm taking three languages this year: Spanish, Russian and German. I want to be a language teacher when I leave school.

b Write the languages under the chart.

Languages

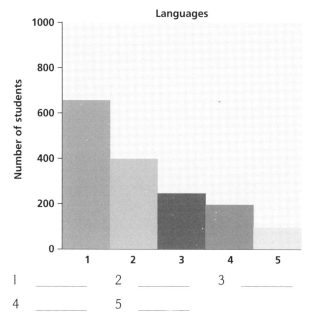

Number of students

1 _____   2 _____   3 _____
4 _____   5 _____

c Are these sentences true (✓) or false (✗)?

1. A lot of schools in England offer five languages. ☐
2. Some students like Spanish because they use it on holiday. ☐
3. French isn't a popular language at the school. ☐
4. You can take an Indian language at this school. ☐
5. Hindi is the new language at the school. ☐
6. The writer is studying three languages. ☐

Writing

2 Use the information in the chart to complete the text about after-school activities.

After-school activities

100%
80%
Football
60%
Film club
Music club
40%
Chess club
20%
History
0%

At our school we can do a lot of after-school activities. A lot of us ¹_____ – about seventy per cent. Of course, the boys like football but a lot of ²_____ play too. After football, about ³_____ _____ are in the ⁴_____ club. In this club, they watch ⁵_____ and then talk about them. It's a very popular club. The ⁶_____ club is also ⁷_____ – about thirty-five per cent ⁸_____ go to this club. Some students like the ⁹_____ , about twenty per cent, but the ¹⁰_____ club isn't popular at all – only about ¹¹_____ of our students go to that club!

Unit 11
Typhoon Opal

1 Where were the members of the OK Club last Saturday? Complete the sentences with *was*, *wasn't*, *were* or *weren't*.

1   Jane and Carol _____were_____ at the cinema. The film _____was_____ brilliant!

2   Ricky _____ at home with his mother on Saturday. They _____ in the garden. His father _____ there because he works on Saturdays.

3   Dave _____ at the shops with his friend, but it _____ seven o'clock and the shops _____ closed.

4   Jack _____ at the bike shop with his brother, but they _____ busy because there _____ any work.

5   Emma _____ at the swimming pool with her sister on Saturday. They _____ happy because a lot of people were there.

2 Match the questions and answers.

1   Who was with Jane at the cinema?   At seven o'clock on Saturday.
2   Where was Ricky?   His brother.
3   When was Dave at the shops?   Because there wasn't any work.
4   Who was with Jack?   Carol.
5   Why weren't they busy?   At the swimming pool.
6   Where was Emma?   In his garden.

3 Answer these questions about yourself.

1   Where were you yesterday at 6 p.m.?

_____

2   Who were you with?

_____

3   Where were you last Saturday at 11 a.m.?

_____

4   Who were you with?

_____

4 Match the phrases in A and B to make sentences with *because*.

A	B
1 It was an interesting story	it was frightened of the storm.
2 My little sister was frightened	the party was very good.
3 We were all happy	it was a hot day.
4 We were very thirsty	the room was very dark.
5 The dog was under the bed	it was true.

1   *It was an interesting story because it was true.*

2   _____

3   _____
    _____

4   _____

5   _____
    _____

5 Match the adjectives with words from the box below to make 'weather' phrases.

rain	sky	storm	sun

1   clear _____   3   violent _____

2   heavy _____   4   warm _____

Survival

1 Imagine this is an interview with Tony Bullimore. Complete the questions.

1 *Were you very frightened* _____ ?

   Yes, I was very frightened and very tired.

2 Did the yacht _____ ?

   No, it didn't go under the water. It went upside-down.

3 Why _____ ?

   It went upside-down because there was an enormous wave in the sea.

4 Where _____ ?

   I went into a small space in the boat, above the water.

5 Did _____ ?

   I had a little chocolate. I was very hungry!

6 Did _____ after the rescue?

   No, I went to a hospital in Australia first. I went on an Australian Navy ship.

7 What about visitors? Did you _____

   _____ ?

   Yes, some reporters, of course, and my wife was there.

8 When _____ ?

   I went home after a few days in hospital.

2 a Find five 'sea' words in Exercise 1.

   1 y _ _ _ _
   2 w _ _ _
   3 b _ _ _
   4 n _ _ _
   5 s _ _ _.

   b Find three 'feelings' words in Exercise 1.

   1 f _ _ _ _ _ _ _ _
   2 t _ _ _ _
   3 h _ _ _ _ _

3 Look at the pictures and complete the story with the past of *be*, *go* or *have* (positive or negative).

Yesterday afternoon at four o'clock Kevin's Mum
¹ _*went*_ to the fridge for some milk but there
² _____ any milk for her coffee! Kevin ³ _____
busy, so he ⁴ _____ to buy some milk for his mother,
but he ⁵ _____ to the shops immediately. He
⁶ _____ to his friend's house first, and they had a
game of football in the park. Then they ⁷ _____ hot
so they ⁸ _____ to a cafe together for some ice
cream. The cafe ⁹ _____ any ice cream,
so they ¹⁰ _____ cola. At half past six they
¹¹ _____ to the shop, but it ¹² _____ open! Kevin
¹³ _____ to his friend's house again, but his friend's
mother ¹⁴ _____ any milk. Then Kevin
¹⁵ _____ home. He ¹⁶ _____ very late and he
¹⁷ _____ any milk. His mother ¹⁸ _____
very angry!

Ricky the spy

1 Complete this diary page with the past tense of *be*, *go* and *have*. Remember to use the negative if necessary.

Today ¹ _was_ a really great day. Mum, Dad, Carol and I ² _____ to the beach for the day. It ³ _____ a good journey because the roads ⁴ _____ very busy and we ⁵ _____ in the car for three hours. In fact, it ⁶ _____ awful!

We ⁷ _____ all very tired after the journey but Carol and I ⁸ _____ swimming in the sea immediately. It ⁹ _____ fantastic! Then we ¹⁰ _____ an enormous lunch of fish and chips in a restaurant. Carol and I ¹¹ _____ a fruit pie after the fish and chips, but Mum and Dad ¹² _____ any pies. Then we ¹³ _____ on a boat trip, but there ¹⁴ _____ some huge waves in the sea and Carol ¹⁵ _____ very well. Mum and Dad ¹⁶ _____ to visit some friends in the evening but Carol and I ¹⁷ _____ with them – we ¹⁸ _____ to the cinema.

2 **a** Jane is asking Carol about her day at the beach. First write Jane's questions.

1 Where/you go yesterday?

Jane: *Where did you go yesterday?*

Carol: _____

2 you/go swimming?

Jane: *Did you go swimming?*

Carol: _____

3 What/you have for lunch?

Jane: _____

Carol: _____

4 you/go home after lunch?

Jane: _____

Carol: _____

5 the boat trip/good?

Jane: _____

Carol: _____

6 Where/you go in the evening?

Jane: _____

Carol: _____

7 your mum and dad/go with you?

Jane: _____

Carol: _____

b Now write Carol's answers. Use the words below to help you.

> fish and chips/fruit pie   no/boat trip
> no/visit some friends   no/huge waves/sea
> to the beach   to the cinema
> yes/in the sea

Example

1 Jane: *Where did you go yesterday?*

Carol: *We went to the beach.*

3 Read the clues. Write the adjectives in the puzzle.

1 very nice
2 Children sometimes feel this in the dark.
3 A typhoon is a very _____ wind.
4 You can be _____ in a town you don't know well.
5 It is a _____ experience when your boat turns upside-down.
6 very, very big
7 You feel this after a long day at school.

1	L							
2	F							
3 S								
			4	L				
		5	T					
		6	E					
			7	T				

What is the hidden word? _____

Skills: story-telling

1 a Read Josie's story of a terrifying experience. Are these sentences true (✓) or false (✗)?

1 Josie's holiday was in a town. ☐
2 She had a frightening holiday. ☐
3 Her father doesn't like boats. ☐

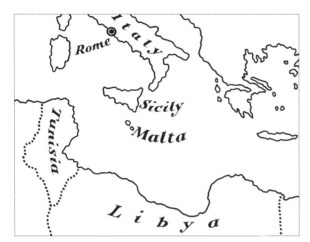

Last year we went on holiday for a week in Italy. My father has a boat there. On Saturday we went by plane to the south of Italy. On Sunday morning we went to the boat and then on Monday we went out on the Mediterranean Sea. Monday and Tuesday were beautiful days – the weather was lovely and we were very relaxed on the boat. On Wednesday Dad had an idea: 'Let's go to Malta; it's only about 200 kilometres from here.' We were nearly at Malta, but then we had some problems. Suddenly there was a strong wind and a violent storm. I was very frightened – some of the waves were enormous – but Dad was quite happy. 'Don't worry. We can stay here and wait for a ship.' We didn't have any food and we didn't have any warm clothes. We were on the sea in this awful weather for two days, and there weren't any other boats. Then, on Friday morning, suddenly the storm went away and the sky was clear. We went back to Italy and then we went to the airport to take a plane home!

b **Write a few notes about each day. Follow the example.**

Saturday: went to *Italy by plane*

Sunday: went to _____

Monday and Tuesday: the weather _____

Wednesday: went to _____

Thursday: the weather _____

Friday: went back to _____

2 Complete Josie's diary.

Saturday	Holiday!
Sunday	We _were on_ the boat all day.
Monday	We _____ the Mediterranean Sea today. It was _____! The weather _____.
Tuesday	We _____ on the boat all day again. The weather _____.
Wednesday	Dad had _____. We went _____. There was a violent _____ and I was _____.
Thursday	Today was really _____! There was another storm, and there weren't any _____ near us.
Friday	This morning the storm _____. We went _____ and then we _____. I don't want to go on Dad's boat again!

Prepare for Unit 12

3 Label the pictures with the underlined words.

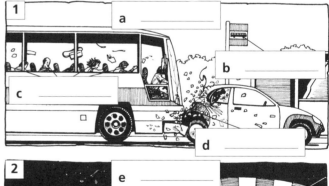

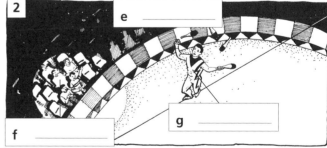

1 There was an <u>accident</u> at the <u>bus-stop</u> last night: a <u>crash</u> between a bus and car. The <u>passengers</u> on the bus were very frightened!

2 We went to the <u>circus</u> yesterday. We had very good <u>seats</u>. The <u>acrobat</u> was really exciting – he went to the top of the tent and did some fantastic tricks.

Unit 12
Lost and found

1 Circle the correct word or words.

1 My friend *arrives*/ *arrived* at six o'clock yesterday.
2 We *didn't*/*don't* enjoy the film last night.
3 What *happened*/*did happened*?
4 How long *waited you*/*did you wait* for the bus?
5 The shop *open*/*opened* at nine o'clock.
6 I *didn't ask*/*not asked* my mother about the circus.
7 Did you *miss*/*missed* the bus last night?
8 She *wants*/*wanted* to go home early yesterday.

2 Correct the statements using the clues.

1 Jane watched a film last night. (no/a video)
   No, Jane didn't watch a film last night. She
   watched a video.

2 Alex liked the acrobats best. (no/horses)
   _____
   _____

3 The lesson started at ten o'clock. (no/half past ten)
   _____
   _____

4 Martin called a friend in London last week. (no/a friend in Paris)
   _____
   _____

5 Julie waited for the bus for twenty minutes. (no/ten minutes)
   _____
   _____

3 Make past simple questions.

1 What time/arrive/at school yesterday?
   What time did you arrive at school yesterday?
2 Who/you/telephone/last night?
   _____
3 What/you/watch/on TV last night?
   _____
4 What/you/like best/on TV last night?
   _____
5 What/you/enjoy/at school yesterday?
   _____

4 **a** Ricky went into town yesterday evening. What did he do? Put the sentences in the correct order (1–6).

a He only watched half the film. It was really awful! ☐
b He waited for a bus. The bus was late. ☐
c The cinema opened at half past six. ☐
d He arrived home at half past nine. ☐
e He arrived at the cinema. It was closed. ☐
f The film started at seven o'clock. ☐

b **Complete Ricky's story.**

Last night Ricky went to the cinema. First, he

[1]_____ for a bus for twenty minutes. The

bus was late. He [2]_____ at the cinema at

six o'clock, but it was [3]_____! It

[4]_____ at half past six. Ricky [5]_____

into the cinema. The film [6]_____ at seven

o'clock and Ricky started to watch it, but it was

[7]_____ and he only [8]_____ half of

it. He [9]_____ out of the cinema and

[10]_____ home at half past nine.

In the news

1 Write the present and past simple forms.

	Present	Past
1	arrive	_____
2	_____	arrested
3	_____	climbed
4	_____	lifted
5	look	_____
6	_____	moved
7	telephone	_____
8	_____	tried
9	wait	_____
10	_____	wanted

2 Read the story. Put the verbs from Exercise 1 in the gaps. Use each verb once.

Mrs Jones had a lot of money. She had a big house with a lovely garden and a very expensive, enormous TV. Bob Smith [1] _wanted_ that TV – he didn't have a TV at all. One day he [2] _____ outside Mrs Jones' house. After half an hour Mrs Jones opened the front door and walked to her car. Bob went to the house and [3] _____ around it. Good – an open window! He [4] _____ in the open window, quietly, and went to the living-room. There was the wonderful TV. He [5] _____ to lift it.

He [6] _____ it a few centimetres on the table, but that was all. He didn't know how to lift it …

Later that day Mrs Jones [7] _____ home from work. On the floor of her living-room was a man – with her TV on his back! She [8] _____ the police. They [9] _____ the television off the man's back easily, but then, of course, they [10] _____ Bob Smith!

3 Correct these sentences about the story.

1 Mrs Jones didn't have much money.
   Mrs Jones had a lot of money. _____

2 Bob Smith wanted her CD player.
   _____

3 One day he waited outside Mrs Jones' office.
   _____

4 Mrs Jones went to work by bus.
   _____

5 Bob went into her house by the front door.
   _____

6 He didn't move the TV.
   _____

7 Mrs Jones telephoned the hospital.
   _____

8 The police helped Bob Smith.
   _____

Come on, Carol!

1 Write these past tense verbs.

1 s a r h c e d   *crashed*
2 r v a r i e d   _____
3 k s a e d   _____
4 s e c r u e d   _____
5 p o s t p e d   _____
6 l l a c e d   _____

2 a   Match the verbs in Exercise 1 with the pictures.

> ## Alan's story

1 _____   2 _____

3 _____   4 _____

5 _____   6 _____

b   Alan is talking to his friend, Neil. First, write past tense verbs in gaps 1–6 in the dialogue.

Alan   I was in town yesterday at Luigi's when two cars [1]_____ in the road.

Neil   Really?

Alan   Yes, really!

Neil   (a) What _____

Alan   I jumped up and [2]_____ a man in the street with a phone …

Neil   Yes …

Alan   … and I [3]_____ the police.

Neil   (b) _____

Alan   Next, I went to the cars and I [4]_____ one of the drivers.

Neil   (c) _____

Alan   Yes, really, it's true! Then the police [5]_____ .

Neil   (d) _____

Alan   Well, they went to the cars, but then a man walked up to me and [6]_____ me to go away.

Neil   What? Why?

Alan   Because it wasn't a real accident. It was only a film and he was the producer!

c   Now write these phrases in gaps (a)–(d) in the dialogue.

> did you do?   What did the police do?
> What happened next?   Really?

3 a   Say these past tense verbs. (Think of the pronunciation of the ending.)

> cleaned   crashed   decided   died   enjoyed
> liked   missed   reported   returned
> stopped   waited   wanted

b   Put the verbs in the correct column.

arrived /d/	asked /t/	started /ɪd/
_____	_____	_____
_____	_____	_____
_____	_____	_____
_____	_____	_____

Skills: news reports

1 Read the three news stories quickly. Match these headlines with the stories.

a   **POLICE FIND MISSING PERFORMER**

b   **125 ESCAPE IN GERMAN AIR DISASTER**

c   **LONDON TOURIST SAVES DOG**

1   A French tourist in London was a hero to one family yesterday. Mr Jacques Lescaux, 22, was in a north London park yesterday afternoon when a frightened little girl asked him: 'Please save my dog. He's in the lake and he can't swim.' Mr Lescaux immediately jumped into the lake.

2   Police arrested circus acrobat Jenny Morgan last night. Two weeks ago Ms Morgan pushed her husband Harry, also an acrobat, to the floor in the middle of a performance. They were ten metres above the ground at the time! The police wanted to question Jenny after the show, but she didn't wait for them.

3   A plane with 125 passengers and crew on board crashed late last night at Berlin airport. Officials at the airport say there wasn't a bomb on the plane and they don't know why it crashed. Reports from Berlin say that all the people survived. Emergency workers rescued the survivors from the plane.

2 Read the texts again and match two of them with these endings.

A   A hundred of the people walked out of the plane and only 25 went to hospital. One passenger talked to us: 'Suddenly there was a loud noise and the plane crashed into some trees outside the airport. It was awful! We're lucky to be alive.'

B   The animal was very frightened but the Frenchman lifted him out of the lake and then called the child's parents. Rover – the dog – was very wet, but he is now safe and well.

3 Complete the ending for the other story. Use the phrases from the box.

> moved to another town   did not find her
> searched the country   tired and hungry
> walked into a police station   wasn't with them
> asked about her husband   to the hospital

The circus _____, but Jenny,

the best acrobat, _____ . The

police _____ for her, but they

_____ . After a few days

Jenny _____

one day and _____ . She

was _____ . The police went

_____ with her when she

visited her husband. Then they arrested her …

Prepare for Unit 13

4   a   Underline eight words for jobs. Use a dictionary.

> critic   direct   silence   environmentalist   farmer
> explorer   filmscript   lawyer   painter   poet
> politician

b   Now circle two words from the world of films. There is one word left. What is it? _____

c   What are these jobs?

1   He or she works with plants and animals, to produce food. _____

2   He or she writes about films. _____

3   He or she makes lovely pictures. _____

4   He or she discusses people's problems in court. _____

5   He or she goes to unusual places in the world. _____

6   He or she makes decisions about his/her country. _____

Unit 13
Behind the camera

1 a Complete the past forms of the verbs with *a, e, i, o* or *u*.

1 w a s/w e r e   6 t _ _ k

2 m _ d _   7 f _ _ n d

3 w _ n   8 k n _ w

4 w r _ t _   9 g _ v _

5 c _ m _   10 s _ w

b Write the past forms from Exercise 1a and their infinitives.

	Infinitive	Past form
1	*be*	*was/were*
2	_____	_____
3	_____	_____
4	_____	_____
5	_____	_____
6	_____	_____
7	_____	_____
8	_____	_____
9	_____	_____
10	_____	_____

2 a Read Susie's diary. Then use the pictures to find six mistakes in the diary. Underline them.

> I was late for school yesterday morning, because I got up late. I had breakfast at half past ten and went to school, but I arrived there at quarter past nine, and my teacher was angry with me. In our English lesson we saw an interesting film on the radio. School finished early and I came home after lunch, in the evening. My friends and I went swimming in the cafe and we found a shark in the water! I came up to my room after supper and wrote a book to my penfriend in America. Then I went to bed.

b Correct the mistakes in Susie's diary.

1 *Susie didn't have breakfast at half past ten. She had breakfast at half past eight.*

2 _____

_____

3 _____

_____

4 _____

_____

5 _____

_____

6 _____

_____

The world of silence

1 Complete this text about Jacques Cousteau. Use the past form of the verbs in the box.

> become   be born   die   fight   invent   make
> play   speak   win   write

Jacques Cousteau [1]_____ in 1910 in France. He
[2]_____ a famous diver and undersea explorer. He
also [3]_____ films about the underwater world, and
one of them – *The World of Silence* – [4]_____ the
top prize at the Cannes Film Festival in 1956.
Cousteau was also an inventor. He [5]_____ the
aqualung with Emile Gagnan in 1943. This gives
undersea divers their own oxygen, so they can stay
under water for a long time. Cousteau was also very
interested in the natural environment and he
[6]_____ for it through all of his life. He always had a
lot of other interests, too: he [7]_____ a few
languages well, he [8]_____ the piano and he
[9]_____ poetry. He [10]_____ in 1997, in Paris.

2 **a** Find these pronouns in the text in Exercise 1.
Which nouns do they refer to?

1   He (line 2)   *Jacques Cousteau*

2   them (line 4)   _____

3   This (line 7)   _____

4   they (line 8)   _____

5   it (line 11)   _____

6   he (line 13)   _____

b Rewrite the sentence with underlined words,
using a pronoun.

Example
My grandfather was fifty when I was born. I first
met my grandfather when he was seventy.

I first met him when he was seventy.

1   My bag is under your chair. Please give my
bag to me.

_____

2   You've got a lot of friends. Let's invite your
friends to the party.

_____

3   My sister was at the cinema yesterday. Did
you see my sister there?

_____

4   John and I want to know your news. Please
tell John and me.

_____

3 **a** What are these jobs? Write the name of the job
under each picture.

1 _____   2 _____

3 _____   4 _____

5 _____   6 _____

b Describe each person's job with these phrases.

> check people's health   design houses   make films
> paint pictures   work for his/her country
> work on a farm

1   *A film director makes films.*

2   _____

3   _____

4   _____

5   _____

6   _____

Chocolate chip cookies

1 Paula's mother was out when she came home from school yesterday. What did she do? Write about each picture.

1 come home from school / half past three / find

   Paula came home from school at half past three

   yesterday. She found a note from her mother.

2 go to her bedroom / put bag / jacket

   _____

   _____

3 go to the kitchen / eat

   _____

   _____

4 go to the living-room / watch

   _____

   _____

5 go back to bedroom / read / not tidy / not do homework

   _____

   _____

6 mother come home / angry

   _____

   _____

2 Answer these questions about yourself.

1 What time did you get up yesterday morning?

   _____

2 What time did you leave school yesterday?

   _____

3 Did you eat any fruit yesterday? What did you eat?

   _____

4 Did your friends give you any presents last year? What?

   _____

3 Complete the sentences with *so* or *because*.

1 Paula was hungry _so_____ she ate all the food.

2 She ate all the food _____ she was greedy!

3 She was lazy _____ she didn't tidy her room.

4 She watched the football _____ she didn't do her homework.

5 Paula's mother was angry _____ she didn't meet her at the bus stop.

6 She was annoyed _____ she didn't give Paula her pocket money.

Skills: inserting new text

1 First read the text about Karen Carter. Then look at sentences 1–4. Match them with letters A–D in the text.

Karen Carter wanted to be a film star from the age of ten, when she saw an old film with Marilyn Monroe. **A** She decided then that she wanted to be beautiful and famous, too. When she was eighteen, she left school and she went to an acting college. She finished the course, but she didn't learn everything she wanted from it. **B** She went to hundreds of interviews for small acting jobs, but she didn't find any interesting work at all. She wanted to copy her favourite film star, too. Her interviewers didn't offer her anything. **C** She didn't have any luck there at first, but after a few months she found a wonderful job! She works in a restaurant where all the waiters and waitresses dress and act as famous film stars! **D**

1   She decided to leave London and to go to Hollywood. _____

2   She wanted to become Marilyn – to walk like her, talk like her, and wear the same clothes. _____

3   She's really happy now and she's not interested in a job in films any more. _____

4   She loved the film and she loved Marilyn Monroe. _____

2 Read the text again with the extra sentences. Answer these questions.

1   Why did Karen decide that she wanted to be beautiful and famous?

_____

2   What did she do when she left school?

_____

3   Did the course give her everything she wanted?

_____

4   Did she find a job that she wanted in London?

_____

5   What kind of job did she find?

_____

Prepare for Unit 14

3 a These are all words for places in a town. Check the meaning of the new ones. Use the Wordlist for Unit 14 on page 80.

bank cafe cinema gallery hostel hotel library market museum restaurant shop theatre zoo

b Put twelve of the words in this word-map.

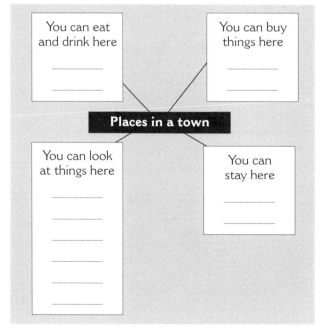

c What is the other word? _____

Write about this place: *You can … here.*

_____

Unit 14
Great journeys

1 Which of these time phrases do we usually use for the present? Which phrases do we usually use for the future? Write them in the lists.

> now   tomorrow   next month   next week
> at the moment   the day after tomorrow

Present

_____

_____

Future

_____

_____

_____

_____

2 a This is a letter from Carol to her penfriend in Canada. Which sentences (1–10) are about the present and which are about the future? Write *P* or *F* by the numbers below.

Thursday 27th May

Dear Helene,

Thanks for your last letter, and thanks for writing in English. ¹I know I'm studying French at school now but I'm afraid my French is still very bad. ²In fact, on Saturday Mum and Dad and I are going to France for a day, so I can practise my French a little. ³We're taking the train from London. ⁴Then we're visiting my grandparents on Sunday.

⁵I'm sitting in my bedroom writing this letter – it's a nice sunny evening here. ⁶Mum and Dad are watching a boring film on TV. ⁷My brother Dave is talking to his girlfriend Jane on the phone – as usual. What do you do in the evenings? ⁸Tomorrow evening I'm playing volleyball with some friends. ⁹Then we're having a pizza together.

¹⁰I'm reading a fantastic book at the moment. It's called 'Captain Corelli's Mandolin'. Do you know it? It's about …

1 _P_   2 _____   3 _____   4 _____   5 _____

6 _____   7 _____   8 _____   9 _____   10 _____

b Write sentences about Carol.

1 At the moment she _____

_____

2 On Friday evening _____

_____

3 On Saturday _____

4 On Sunday _____

_____

3 a Find six jobs.

writer
inventor producer business
explorer teacher man

b Where do the people from Exercise 3a work? Complete the sentences.

1 A _____ usually works in an office.

2 A _____ usually works in a school.

3 An _____ often works in a workshop.

4 A _____ often works in a studio.

5 A _____ often works at home.

6 An _____ travels to different places.

4 a Say these words.

> adventure   window   worried   clever   how
> move   relative   swap   write   why

b Eight of the words have the /w/ (<u>w</u>as) sound or the /v/ (ha<u>v</u>e) sound. Write them in the lists. (Be careful – two words do not have these sounds!)

was /w/   **have** /v/

_____   _____

_____   _____

_____   _____

_____   _____

On the town

1 You want to go out this evening. Complete the suggestions using the places in brackets '( )' and a verb from the box.

go	have	visit	watch	go

1 (theatre) Perhaps we can *go to the theatre.*

2 (pizza) Let's _____

3 (film) How about _____

4 (wax museum) Shall we _____

_____

5 (disco) Why don't we _____

_____

2 Write suggestions about the activities in the pictures. Use a different type of suggestion for each activity.

1   go to

2   have

4   play

3   go

5   visit

1 Why _____

2 Perhaps _____

3 How _____

4 _____

5 _____

3 a   Find ten places in a town.

sta	hos	lib	cine	fe	aurant	ma	nk
rest	the	ba	ca	ery	atre	tel	rary
z	gall			tion	oo		

station _____   _____   _____

_____   _____   _____

_____

b   Complete the text with six of the places.

Last weekend I visited London with some friends. We arrived at the train [1]_____ on Friday evening and we stayed in a [2]_____. On Saturday morning we went to the [3]_____ and saw some interesting animals. Then, in the afternoon, we went to a show at a [4]_____. I saw my favourite actor! After the show we had dinner in an expensive [5]_____. It was delicious! On Sunday morning we visited an enormous art [6]_____. It had a lot of lovely pictures. Then we took our train home. It was a great weekend!

4 Rewrite this dialogue with the correct punctuation. Look for:

10 mistakes with capital letters (A, B, C)
7 mistakes with full stops (.)
5 mistakes with apostrophes (')
2 mistakes with question marks (?).

Ellen what shall we do tomorrow afternoon

Luke i dont know how about going swimming

Ellen no, i dont think so im playing badminton in the morning

Luke perhaps we can go shopping

Ellen i havent got any money lets watch a video

Luke yes, good idea

Ellen *What shall we do tomorrow afternoon?*

Luke _____

_____

Ellen _____

_____

Luke _____

Ellen _____

Luke _____

Plans for a party

1   a   First complete the suggestions (1–6) in the dialogue. Use the pictures to help you.

Mike   What shall I do for my birthday this year?

Chris   I know. Why don't we have a barbecue?

Mike   **A** _____ 😄

Chris   What shall we have to eat?

Mike   Let's ¹ _have some hamburgers._

Chris   **B** _____ 😄

          What shall we have to drink?

Mike   Why ² _____ ?

Chris   **C** _____ 🙁

          A lot of people don't like them.

Mike   OK. We can ³ _____ ,

          too.

Chris   **D** _____ 😄

Mike   What shall we do about music?

Chris   ⁴ _____ ask

          Jo to bring _____ ?

Mike   Her guitar? **E** _____

          Do you think she wants to play her guitar

          all afternoon? ⁵ _____

          take _____ .

          to the park.

Chris   OK. Who shall we invite?

Mike   ⁶ _____

          all the students from our class at school?

Chris   **F** _____ 😄

          Let's start phoning them now!

b   Now complete A–F with sentences from the box. Use the pictures to help you.

> Oh yes, I love hamburgers!   Yes, why not?
> I'm not sure.   Oh no! I hate milkshakes!
> Great idea! I love barbecues!
> Yes, a lot of people like cola.

2   Mike is writing a letter about the barbecue to another friend. Complete the letter with information from the dialogue.

> Dear Keith
>
> I'm writing to tell you that I'm ¹ _____ a barbecue for my ² _____ this year. It's on Saturday 14th. Would you like to come?
>
> We're ³ _____ hamburgers to eat, and milkshakes and ⁴ _____ to drink. We're ⁵ _____ the ⁶ _____ to the park. I'm ⁷ _____ all my friends from school.
>
> I hope you can come.
>
> Mike

3   You and some friends want to plan something for another friend's birthday. Use the pictures to write five suggestions.

1 _____

2 _____

3 _____

4 _____

5 _____

Skills: writing about plans

1 You are going to London for the weekend. Here are your notes about what you can do. Underline five things you would like to do.

> VISIT TO LONDON, 14TH–16TH OCTOBER
>
> (Arrive on Friday at 6.00 p.m. Leave on Sunday at 2.00 p.m.)
>
> <u>Shopping</u>
> Oxford Street (main shopping street) all day on Saturday.
> Covent Garden (market – some things quite cheap) all day on Saturday, some shops and stalls open on Sunday.
>
> <u>Museums</u>
> The London Dungeon (frightening!) 10.00–6.00 every day.
> Madame Tussaud's (famous wax museum) 10.00–5.30 every day.
>
> <u>Sights</u>
> The Tower of London (historical) 9.00–5.00.
> Buckingham Palace (royal family) 9.30–4.15 summer only.
> London Zoo (huge zoo, lots of animals) 10.00–5.00
> Boat trip on the river (centre of London) every hour.
>
> <u>Shows</u>
> Rock Circus (wax rock stars, music) 11.00–9.00 every day.
> The Planetarium (space, etc.) 12.00–6.00
>
> <u>Cinemas</u>
> Lots of cinemas in the centre, usually 4 or 5 performances a day, last one usually at about 9.00 p.m.

2 Organize your weekend. Write your activities in the correct place.

Friday evening: _____

Saturday morning: _____

Saturday afternoon: _____

Saturday evening: _____

Sunday morning: _____

3 Complete this letter to a friend and tell him/her what you are doing in London for the weekend.

> Dear _____
>
> I'm going to London next weekend! It's very exciting. I'm arriving at six o'clock on Friday evening and then I'm _____
> _____
>
> On Saturday morning I'm _____
>
> and in the afternoon I'm _____
>
> Then, in the evening I'm _____
> _____
>
> Unfortunately, I'm leaving London at two o'clock on Sunday but in the morning I'm _____
> _____

Prepare for Unit 15

4 **a** Write the words for these things. Use the Wordlist for Unit 15 on page 80.

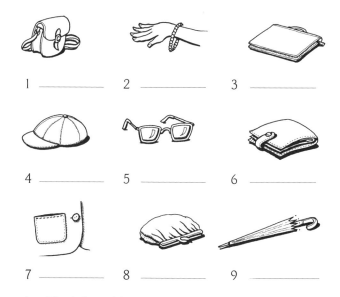

1 _____ 2 _____ 3 _____

4 _____ 5 _____ 6 _____

7 _____ 8 _____ 9 _____

b Find the odd one out in these lists.

1 We wear these things:
 cap   bracelet   glasses   purse

2 We carry these things:
 briefcase   bag   umbrella   glasses

3 We put money in these things:
 wallet   purse   umbrella   pocket

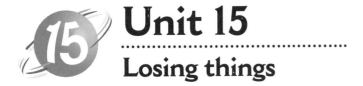

Unit 15

Losing things

1 a Write the offers from the box under the pictures (A).

> Can I take your dog for a walk?
> Let me carry your briefcase.
> I'll pay for your coffee.
> Shall I help you with your homework?

b Write a response to each offer (B). Use the pictures to help you.

A _____

B _____

A _____

B _____

A _____

B _____

A _____

B _____

2 Make different offers from the jumbled words.

1 I bring now shall it ?
Shall I bring it now?

2 help you I can ?

_____

3 that you I'll for do .

_____

4 bag let your carry me .

_____

5 open I door the shall ?

_____

6 the I'll phone answer .

_____

3 a Find fifteen words or phrases.

credit card, drum, _____

_____

_____

More mix-ups

1 Complete the lists of possessive pronouns and adjectives.

Personal pronouns	Possessive adjective	Possessive pronoun
I	*my*	_____
you	_____	_____
he	_____	_____
she	_____	_____
it	_____	*its*
we	_____	_____
you	*your*	_____
they	_____	_____

2 Complete the speech bubbles in each cartoon. Use the words and phrases from the box.

> his   mine   mine   my friend's   ours
> theirs   theirs   yours   whose

1 Chicken and chips. _____ is this?

I think it's _____.

2 Two coffees. Are they _____?

Yes, they're _____.

3 Is this your jacket, Madam?

No, it's not _____. It's _____.

4 Did you order a pizza, sir?

No, I didn't! It's _____!

5 This bottle of water. I think it's _____.

No, it's _____.

3 Read this dialogue between the boy and the waiter. Change the underlined words to *one* or *ones*.

Waiter   Can I take your order?
Boy   Yes, can I have a pizza with mushrooms please?
Waiter   I'm sorry, we haven't got any mushroom [1]<u>pizzas</u>.
Boy   Well, can I have [2]<u>a pizza</u> with chicken, please?
Waiter   I'm sorry, we haven't got any chicken [3]<u>pizzas</u>.
Boy   Well, what about [4]<u>a pizza</u> with olives?
Waiter   I'm sorry, we haven't …
Boy   OK, OK. What kind of pizzas have you got, then?
Waiter   We've got cheese and tomato pizzas.
Boy   All right. I'll have a cheese and tomato [5]<u>pizza</u>.

1 _____   2 _____   3 _____
4 _____   5 _____

4 a   Say these words.

> bra<u>c</u>elet   lo<u>s</u>e   di<u>s</u>appear   politi<u>c</u>ian   gla<u>ss</u>
> pu<u>sh</u>   situa<u>ti</u>on   si<u>z</u>e   <u>s</u>teak   who<u>s</u>e   <u>z</u>oo

b   Which sound do the underlined letters have? Put them in the correct column in the chart.

see /s/	**as** /z/	**show** /ʃ/
_____	_____	_____
_____	_____	_____
_____	_____	_____
_____	_____	_____

The OK Club on TV

1 Complete the sentences.

1 It's my book. It's *mine*____ .

2 This is _____ house. It belongs to us.

3 This bike belongs to John. It's _____ new bike.

4 'Mum, Dad - whose photos are these? They're awful!'

'Oh dear. They're _____ . We took them years ago!'

5 'Which one is John and Penny's new car?'

'This one is _____ .'

6 'What's this? Is it _____ ?'

'Yes, it's my essay.'

7 'Oh, dear. Which one is _____ ?'

'I think this one belongs to her.'

8 'Does this dictionary belong to you?'

'Yes, it's _____ .'

2 Put apostrophes in the correct places.

1 Its Rickys waistcoat.

2 Its the film crews camera.

3 Theyre the club members biscuits.

4 Its the clubs back entrance.

5 Hes Carols brother.

6 Shes Carols mother.

3 Jane is showing you around the OK Club.
Complete the dialogue using the ideas in the box.

> Yes, I'd like to become a member.
> Yes, please. Can I have one with milk and sugar?
> Thanks. I'd love to meet them.
> OK. I live at …   Thank you.
> Yes, I'd like that.   No, thank you. I'm not hungry.
> I'm sorry, there isn't a film in it.

Jane Hi. Welcome to the OK Club. Here, I'll take your coat.

You _____

Jane Shall I show you around?

You _____

Jane Let me introduce you to the other members.

You _____

Jane Shall I make you a coffee?

You _____

Jane Yes, of course. Can I get you something to eat? We've got sandwiches.

You _____

Jane Oh, you've got your camera. I'll take a photo of you here.

You _____

Jane OK. Would you like to join the club? Shall I get you a membership form?

You _____

Jane Thanks for coming. Let me take your address and I'll tell you when we have a party.

You _____

4 Make offers for these situations.

1 Your teacher has got a lot of books in his hands and he can't open the door.

Let me _____

2 It's very hot in the classroom. All the students are hot.

Shall I _____ ?

3 Your brother wants some crisps but he is writing an important essay and can't go to the shop.

I'll _____

4 A Japanese tourist is looking at a map in the street. You think she is lost.

Can _____ ?

5 Your mother and father are very tired and they don't want to cook supper.

_____

6 You and your friend are at the cinema. Your friend hasn't got any money with her, but you've got some money.

_____

Skills: vocabulary round-up

1 a   Divide the words in the box into eight groups of three words each. Write them in the correct group in the word-map.

b   Write two more words for each group. Use your vocabulary notebook to help you.

apricots   armchair   bank   basketball   bed
cinema   cold   elephant   farmer   fox   giraffe
hamburger   jeans   judo   lawyer   museum
potato   shirt   shop assistant   table   sunny
swimming   trainers   windy

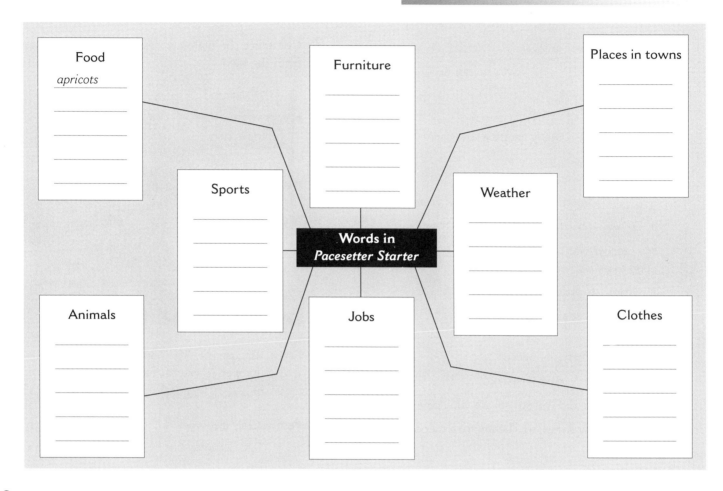

2 Choose one word from each group and write a sentence about it.

Example

Food: *Apricots are my favourite fruit.*

Food: _____

_____

Furniture: _____

_____

Places in town: _____

_____

Sports: _____

_____

Weather: _____

_____

Animals: _____

_____

Jobs: _____

_____

Clothes: _____

_____

Consolidation

Check yourself

Grammar

1 Choose the correct answer.

1 The weather _____ awful on our holiday last week.

   a was   **b** is   **c** were

2 There _____ many people at the party when I arrived.

   a hasn't   **b** weren't   **c** wasn't

3 _____ a good time at the barbecue yesterday?

   a Did you   **b** Had you   **c** Did you have

4 My teacher was pleased because I _____ a good essay last week.

   a wrote   **b** write   **c** writed

5 Why did he eat all the sandwiches? _____ he was hungry!

   a So   **b** When   **c** Because

6 What _____ next weekend?

   a do you   **b** did you do   **c** are you doing

7 Today's Friday so we aren't coming to school _____!

   a tomorrow   **b** today   **c** yesterday

8 _____ go to the market on Saturday?

   a Let's   **b** Shall we   **c** How about

9 That bag is very heavy. Here, _____ carry it.

   a can I   **b** let me   **c** shall I

10 I'm sorry, but we've got the tickets for those seats. They're _____!

   a our   **b** us   **c** ours

   /10

2 Complete the dialogue. Use words and phrases from the box.

did she buy   didn't have   didn't look   first   gave
Let me   one   ours   Shall I get   wanted

Peter Excuse me. My mother [1]_____ me this jumper. I'd like to change it.

Lois Certainly. When [2]_____ it?

Peter Only last week. I [3]_____ to return it last Saturday but I [4]_____ time.

Lois That's fine. Is there a problem with the jumper?

Peter No, not really, but I don't like the colour. I'd like a blue [5]_____.

Lois OK. [6]_____ you a blue one, or would you like to have a look at some other jumpers?

Peter No, can you just give me a blue one, please?

Lois Oh, hang on a minute. This jumper isn't [7]_____. It's from another shop, Berry's.

Peter Oh, I am sorry. I [8]_____ at the bag carefully. Where Berry's?

Lois It's in the High Street, but wait a minute. [9]_____ phone them [10]_____. I think they're closed on Thursdays.

   /10

70

Vocabulary

3 Write the names of the objects in the picture.

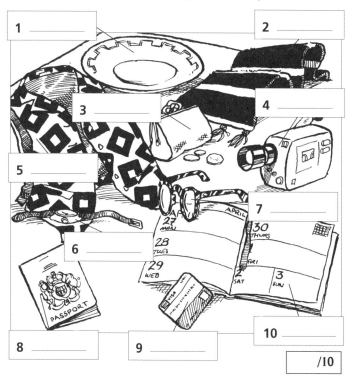

1 _____
2 _____
3 _____
4 _____
5 _____
6 _____
7 _____
8 _____
9 _____
10 _____

/10

Communication

4 Match A and B.

A
1 Why did she eat all the chips?
2 Did you see the acrobats?
3 What happened next?
4 What happened at the end?
5 Shall we go to the cinema tonight?
6 Why don't we have a pizza?
7 What are you wearing tomorrow?
8 How did you feel when you arrived?
9 Let me carry your bag.
10 Can I help you?

B
a Next, we all went to our seats.
b Oh, just jeans and a shirt.
c Yes, I'd like to see the new Matt Damon film.
d I was really tired!
e Sorry, but I'm not hungry.
f Because she was hungry.
g Well, finally, they all went home.
h Yes. I'm looking for a present for my mother.
i No, I didn't.
j Thanks. It's very heavy.

1 ___ 2 ___ 3 ___ 4 ___ 5 ___
6 ___ 7 ___ 8 ___ 9 ___ 10 ___

/10

Pronunciation

5 a Which word in each list has the same sound as the example word? Underline it.

1 <u>wa</u>ve: van how weather write
2 <u>vi</u>deo: wallet funny wave theme
3 <u>s</u>ink: lazy desert sight shall
4 <u>sh</u>elf: Spanish unusual scarf zoo
5 la<u>z</u>y: style ours promise squid

b Say these past tense verbs to yourself, then put them in the correct column in the chart.

belonged   booked   hated   hoped
painted   returned

asked /t/	**joined** /d/	**wanted** /ɪd/
	belonged	

/10

Total	/50

Review

6 Look at Units 11–15 of your Student's Book again. Add any new words to the charts on pages 73–76 of this book.

7 Do you remember the lessons from Units 11–15? Look at your scores ans complete the chart for yourself.

I remember ...

	60%–100% ★ ★★	40%–60% ★ ★☆	0%–40% ★ ☆☆
Grammar			
Vocabulary			
Communication			
Pronunciation			

Skills: a news story

Reading

1 a Look at these two pictures. Match four words from the box with each picture.

girl cat beach boat boys climb sea tree

1: _____ _____ _____ _____

2: _____ _____ _____ _____

b Read the story quickly. Check your words. Which picture goes with the story? ___

Jill Stiles rescued a child from the sea last week. Jill was on Brighton beach with her family, when she saw a small child in the sea. She didn't know what to do, but she thought for a few minutes and she had an idea. First, she found a small boat and went out to the little girl in it. Next, she pulled the girl into the boat and took her back to the beach. The little girl's family was now on the beach. They were worried because their little girl wasn't there. Jill found the family and returned their child to them. They were really happy!

2 Answer the questions about the story.

1 What did Jill do?
   She rescued a child from the sea.

2 When did she do it?
   _____

3 Where was she?
   _____

4 Who was she with?
   _____

5 What did she see?
   _____

6 What did she do first?
   _____

7 What did she do next?
   _____

8 What did she do at the end?
   _____

9 How did the family feel?
   _____

Writing

3 Complete this text about the rescue in the other picture. Use the questions and answers to help you.

- What did Joe do?   He rescued a cat from a tree.
- When did he do it?   Yesterday.
- Where was he?   In his garden.
- Who was he with?   A friend.
- What did he hear?   He heard an unusual sound.
- What did he do first?   He found a box and climbed into the tree.
- What did he do next?   He took the cat and carried it down.
- What did he do at the end?   He phoned the number around the cat's neck.
- How did the woman feel?   She was very pleased.

Joe Black rescued [1]_____ from a [2]_____. Joe was in [3]_____ with [4]_____, when he heard [5]_____. He didn't know what to do, but he thought for a few minutes and he had an idea. First, he found a [6]_____ and he used it to [7]_____. Next, he took the cat and [8]_____. He gave it some fish and some milk. Then he noticed something around the cat's neck – it was a piece of paper with a phone number on it! He [9]_____ and he spoke to a woman. It was her cat! He took the cat to her house. She was [10]_____!

Vocabulary

List and translation

Complete this list of things in the classroom from page 15 of your Student's Book. Translate them.

English	My language
bag	
book	
chair	
desk	

Add more things from the classroom to the list when you learn new words.

Picture dictionary

Label the pictures of parts of the body.

eyes

Add more labels to the pictures when you learn new words.

Word-maps

Word-map 1: _____

Complete word-map 1 with the words from page 26 Exercise 2 in your Student's Book.

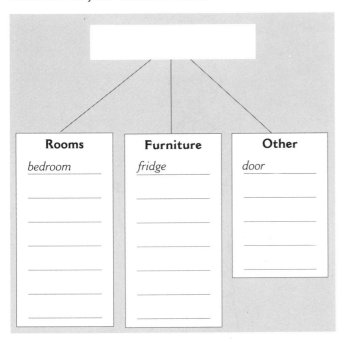

Add more words to the word-map when you learn them.

Word-map 2: clothes

Complete word-map 2 with the words from page 28 Exercise 1 in your Student's Book.

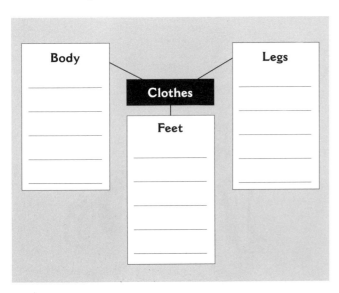

Add more words to the word-map when you learn them.

Word-chart 1: things in a home

Write the things in different rooms in a home.

Room	What's in it?
Kitchen	_cooker, fridge_
Living-room	_sofa_
Dining-room	_table_
Bedroom	
Bathroom	
Garage	

Word-chart 2: adjectives

Write the opposites of the adjectives.

Adjective	Opposite
small	_big, large_
fantastic	
short	
curly	
fair	
true	

Add more adjectives to the list when you learn them.

Map: countries, nationalities, languages

Write the countries on the map when you learn them. Complete
the chart with nationalities and languages.

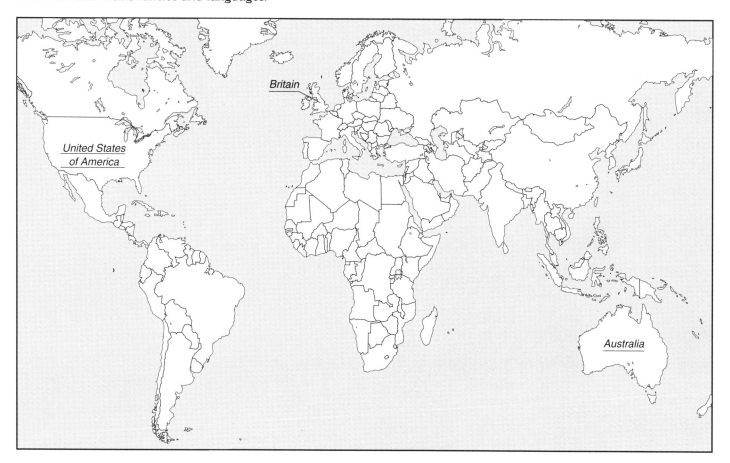

Country	Nationality	Main Language(s)
Britain	British	English
United States of America	American	English

Word family tree: food

Write food words in this word family tree.

```
                    FOOD
       ┌──────┬───────┼───────┬──────┐
     meat    fish  vegetables fruit  other
       │      │        │       │      │
     lamb    tuna   potatoes  apple  bread
     ___     ___     ___      ___    ___
     ___     ___     ___      ___    ___
     ___     ___     ___      ___    ___
                     ___      ___    ___
                     ___
```

Add more words to this family tree when you learn them.

Word family: sport

Complete the chart with nouns and verbs from Unit 8.

Noun	Verb
swimming	swim
football	play football
aerobics	do aerobics
_____	_____
_____	_____
_____	_____
_____	_____
_____	_____
_____	_____
_____	_____

Add more words for sport to this chart when you learn them.

Wordlist

Preliminary pages

a /ə/
again /ə'gen/
at /æt, ət/
Australia /ɒ'streɪliə/
bank /bæŋk/
basketball /'bɑ:skɪtbɔ:l/
Britain /'brɪtən/
cafe /'kæfeɪ/
Canada /'kænədə/
cassette /kə'set/
cinema /'sɪnəmə/
coffee /'kɒfi/
cola /'kəʊlə/
computer /kəm'pju:tə(r)/
do /du:/
doctor /'dɒktə(r)/
example /ɪg'zɑ:mpl/
excuse me /ɪk'skju:z mi:/
football /'fʊtbɔ:l/
good morning /gʊd 'mɔ:nɪŋ/
goodbye /gʊd'baɪ/
hamburger /'hæmbɜ:gə(r)/
hotel /həʊ'tel/
I /aɪ/
it /ɪt/
Japan /dʒə'pæn/
lemonade /lemə'neɪd/
listen /'lɪsn/
look at /'lʊk æt, ət/
mean /mi:n/
museum /mju:'zɪəm/
no /nəʊ/
park /pɑ:k/
partner /'pɑ:tnə(r)/
picture /'pɪktʃə(r)/
pizza /'pi:tsə/
please /pli:z/
policeman /pə'li:smən/
read /ri:d/
restaurant /'restrɒnt/
sandwich /'sændwɪtʃ/
say /seɪ/
secretary /'sekrətri/
taxi /'tæksi/
telephone (n) /'telɪfəʊn/
television /telɪ'vɪʒn/
tennis /'tenɪs/
thank you /'θæŋk ju:/
that's right / wrong /ðæts
 'raɪt, 'rɒŋ/
the /ðə/
this /ðɪs/
train (n) /treɪn/
understand /ʌndə'stænd/
university /ju:nɪ'vɜ:səti/
use /ju:z/
video /'vɪdiəʊ/
volleyball /'vɒlibɔ:l/
what /wɒt/

work with /'wɜ:k wɪð/
write /raɪt/
wrong /rɒŋ/
yacht /jɒt/
yes /jes/
you /ju:/

Unit 1

address /ə'dres/
and /ænd, ənd/
Argentina /ɑ:dʒən'ti:nə/
be /bi:/
Brazil /brə'zɪl/
brother /'brʌðə(r)/
careful /'keəfl/
club /klʌb/
eight /eɪt/
England /'ɪŋglənd/
fax /fæks/
family /'fæməli/
fine /faɪn/
five /faɪv/
for /fɔ:(r), fə(r)/
four /fɔ:(r)/
from /frɒm, frəm/
Greece /gri:s/
he /hi:/
hello /he'ləʊ/
her /hɜ:(r)/
here /hɪə(r)/
hi /haɪ/
his /hɪz/
how /haʊ/
Hungary /'hʌŋgəri/
in /ɪn/
later /'leɪtə(r)/
look out! /lʊk 'aʊt/
me /mi:/
meet /mi:t/
message /'mesɪdʒ/
Mexico /'meksɪkəʊ/
my /maɪ/
name /neɪm/
new /nju:/
nine /naɪn/
number /'nʌmbə(r)/
OK /əʊ'keɪ/
one /wʌn/
phone (v) /fəʊn/
pleased /pli:zd/
Poland /'pəʊlənd/
really /'rɪəli/
seven /'sevn/
she /ʃi:/
six /sɪks/
sorry /'sɒri/
Spain /speɪn/
ten /ten/
thanks /θæŋks/
three /θri:/

to /tu:, tə/
Turkey /'tɜ:ki/
two /tu:/
United States /ju:naɪtɪd 'steɪts/
very /'veri/
we /wi:/
well /wel/
where /weə(r)/
your /jɔ:(r)/

Unit 2
about /ə'baʊt/
Africa /'æfrɪkə/
agent /'eɪdʒənt/
America /ə'merɪkə/
an /æn, ən/
animal /'ænɪml/
ant /ænt/
bag /bæg/
bird /bɜ:d/
book (n) /bʊk/
boy /bɔɪ/
chair /tʃeə(r)/
city /'sɪti/
come /kʌm/
country /'kʌntri/
desk /desk/
eighteen /eɪ'ti:n/
elephant /'elɪfənt/
eleven /ɪ'levn/
evening /'i:vnɪŋ/
fifteen /fɪf'ti:n/
(on) fire /(ɒn) 'faɪə(r)/
fish /fɪʃ/
fourteen /fɔ:'ti:n/
France /fra:ns/
friend /frend/
girl /gɜ:l/
great /greɪt/
help /help/
How old ...? /haʊ 'əʊld/
insect /'ɪnsekt/
kettle /'ketl/
know /nəʊ/
man /mæn/
member /'membə(r)/
nineteen /naɪn'ti:n/
not /nɒt/
old /əʊld/
operation /ɒpə'reɪʃn/
pen /pen/
pencil /'pensl/
people /'pi:pl/
poster /'pəʊstə(r)/
Scotland /'skɒtlənd/
see (you) /si: (ju:)/
seventeen /sevn'ti:n/
shark /ʃa:k/
sister /'sɪstə(r)/
sixteen /sɪks'ti:n/
smile /smaɪl/
story /'stɔ:ri/

student /'stju:dənt/
table /'teɪbl/
they /ðeɪ/
thirteen /θɜ:'ti:n/
together /tə'geðə(r)/
too /tu:/
twelve /twelv/
twenty /'twenti/
welcome /'welkəm/
Well done! /wel 'dʌn/
who /hu:/
worry /'wʌri/
woman /'wʊmən/
young /jʌŋ/

Unit 3
arm /a:m/
Asia /'eɪʒə/
awful /'ɔ:fl/
big /bɪg/
black /blæk/
blue /blu:/
body /'bɒdi/
brain /breɪn/
brown /braʊn/
bus /bʌs/
but /bʌt, bət/
cat /kæt/
chance /tʃa:ns/
change /tʃeɪndʒ/
Central America /sentrəl ə'merɪkə/
colour /'kʌlə(r)/
curly /'kɜ:li/
dark /da:k/
different /'dɪfrənt/
dog /dɒg/
dream /dri:m/
ear /ɪə(r)/
Europe /'jʊərəp/
eye /aɪ/
fair /feə(r)/
false /fɔ:ls, fɒls/
fantastic /fæn'tæstɪk/
father /'fa:ðə(r)/
forest /'fɒrɪst/
fox /fɒks/
frog /frɒg/
glass lizard /gla:s 'lɪzəd/
giraffe /dʒɪ'ra:f/
good /gʊd/
grandfather /'grænfa:ðə(r)/
grandmother /'grænmʌðə(r)/
green /gri:n/
grey /greɪ/
guess (n) /ges/
hair /heə(r)/
has / have got /hæz (həz), hæv (həv) gɒt/
head /hed/
him /hɪm/
idea /aɪ'dɪə/

leg /leg/
like (what's he ...) /laɪk/
living /'lɪvɪŋ/
long /lɒŋ/
lucky /'lʌki/
maybe /'meɪbi/
mess /mes/
money /'mʌni/
mother /'mʌðə(r)/
moustache /mə'sta:ʃ/
mouth /maʊθ/
neck /nek/
north /nɔ:θ/
nose /nəʊz/
now /naʊ/
orange /'ɒrɪndʒ/
paint /peɪnt/
pence /pens/
penny /'peni/
pet /pet/
place /pleɪs/
problem /'prɒbləm/
red /red/
same /seɪm/
school /sku:l/
short /ʃɔ:t/
small /smɔ:l/
snake /sneɪk/
so /səʊ/
spider /'spaɪdə(r)/
straight /streɪt/
summer /'sʌmə(r)/
tail /teɪl/
tall /tɔ:l/
their /ðeə(r)/
think /θɪŋk/
time /taɪm/
tree /tri:/
true /tru:/
wall /wɔ:l/
white /waɪt/
winter /'wɪntə(r)/
yellow /'jeləʊ/

Unit 4
also /'ɔ:lsəʊ/
all /ɔ:l/
all right /'ɔ:l raɪt/
amazing /ə'meɪzɪŋ/
apartment /ə'pa:tmənt/
armchair /'a:mtʃeə(r)/
bad /bæd/
ball /bɔ:l/
basin /'beɪsən/
bathroom /'ba:θrʊm, -ru:m/
bed /bed/
bedroom /'bedrʊm, -ru:m/
boring /'bɔ:rɪŋ/
car /ka:(r)/
clothes /kləʊðz/
cooker /'kʊkə(r)/
date (appointment) /deɪt/

dining-room /'daɪnɪŋ rʊm, ru:m/
door /dɔ:(r)/
excuse (n) /ɪk'skju:s/
fan /fæn/
favourite /'feɪvrɪt/
film /fɪlm/
fridge /frɪdʒ/
garage /'gærɪdʒ, 'gæra:ʒ/
gold /gəʊld/
hand /hænd/
happy /'hæpi/
helmet /'helmɪt/
holidays /'hɒlɪdeɪz/
home /həʊm/
house /haʊs/
jeans /dʒi:nz/
jumper /'dʒʌmpə(r)/
kitchen /'kɪtʃɪn/
lake /leɪk/
large /la:dʒ/
living-room /'lɪvɪŋ rʊm, ru:m/
loud /laʊd/
millionaire /mɪljə'neə(r)/
modern /'mɒdn/
near /nɪə(r)/
next to /'neks tu:, tə/
on /ɒn/
our /'aʊə(r)/
outside /'aʊtsaɪd/
pair /peə(r)/
person /'pɜ:sn/
plan (n) /plæn/
plant /pla:nt/
player /'pleɪə(r)/
radio /'reɪdiəʊ/
room /rʊm, ru:m/
Saturday /'sætədeɪ/
save /seɪv/
sell /sel/
shirt /ʃɜ:t/
shoes /ʃu:z/
shower /'ʃaʊə(r)/
sink (n) /sɪŋk/
skirt /skɜ:t/
socks /sɒks/
sofa /'səʊfə/
some /sʌm, səm/
sometimes /'sʌmtaɪmz/
street /stri:t/
sweatshirt /'swetʃɜ:t/
swim /swɪm/
swimming pool /'swɪmɪŋ pu:l/
team /ti:m/
then /ðen/
there is / are /ðeər ɪz, a:(r)/
thing /θɪŋ/
toilet /'tɔɪlət/
town /taʊn/
trainers /'treɪnəz/
trousers /'traʊzəz/
T-shirt /'ti: ʃɜ:t/

tomorrow /təˈmɒrəʊ/
under /ˈʌndə(r)/
up /ʌp/
usual /ˈjuːʒʊəl/
visitor /ˈvɪzɪtə(r)/
watch (v) /wɒtʃ/
window /ˈwɪndəʊ/

Unit 5

another /əˈnʌðə(r)/
any /ˈeni/
apple /ˈæpl/
ask /ɑːsk/
banana /bəˈnɑːnə/
beef /biːf/
bike /baɪk/
bread /bred/
carrot /ˈkærət/
cent /sent/
cheese /tʃiːz/
cherry /ˈtʃeri/
chicken /ˈtʃɪkɪn/
chillies /ˈtʃɪliz/
chips /tʃɪps/
chocolate /ˈtʃɒklət/
choose /tʃuːz/
coconut /ˈkəʊkənʌt/
cold /kəʊld/
cook /kʊk/
coriander /kɒriˈændə(r)/
cow /kaʊ/
count /kaʊnt/
delicious /dɪˈlɪʃəs/
dish /dɪʃ/
drink /drɪŋk/
eat /iːt/
egg /eg/
eighty /ˈeɪti/
enjoy /ɪnˈdʒɔɪ/
extra /ˈekstrə/
famous /ˈfeɪməs/
fifty /ˈfɪfti/
food /fuːd/
forty /ˈfɔːti/
fruit /fruːt/
garlic /ˈgɑːlɪk/
hot /hɒt/
(a) hundred /(ə) ˈhʌndrəd/
ice /aɪs/
ice cream /aɪs ˈkriːm/
important /ɪmˈpɔːtənt/
information /ɪnfəˈmeɪʃn/
international /ɪntəˈnæʃənl/
juice /dʒuːs/
ketchup /ˈketʃʌp/
lamb /læm/
lemon /ˈlemən/
lettuce /ˈletɪs/
like /laɪk/
list /lɪst/
(a) lot (of) /(ə) ˈlɒt (əv)/
love /lʌv/

main /meɪn/
meal /miːl/
meat /miːt/
milk /mɪlk/
milkshake /ˈmɪlkʃeɪk/
mineral water /ˈmɪnərəl
  wɔːtə(r)/
mushroom /ˈmʌʃrʊm, -ruːm/
mustard /ˈmʌstəd/
ninety /ˈnaɪnti/
oil /ɔɪl/
olive /ˈɒlɪv/
onion /ˈʌnjən/
only /ˈəʊnli/
order (n & v) /ˈɔːdə(r)/
other /ˈʌðə(r)/
pear /peə(r)/
pie /paɪ/
pig /pɪg/
pork /pɔːk/
potatoes /pəˈteɪtəʊz/
pound /paʊnd/
programme /ˈprəʊgræm/
pudding /ˈpʊdɪŋ/
recipe /ˈresəpi/
rice /raɪs/
roast /rəʊst/
salt /sɔːlt, sɒlt/
sauce /sɔːs/
sausage /ˈsɒsɪdʒ/
secret /ˈsiːkrət/
seventy /ˈsevnti/
sixty /ˈsɪksti/
sort /sɔːt/
spice, spicy /spaɪs, -i/
strawberry /ˈstrɔːbri/
sugar /ˈʃʊgə(r)/
tea /tiː/
teach /tiːtʃ/
these /ðiːz/
thick /θɪk/
thin /θɪn/
thirty /ˈθɜːti/
today /təˈdeɪ/
tomato /təˈmɑːtəʊ/
tuna /ˈtjuːnə/
vanilla /vəˈnɪlə/
vegetable /ˈvedʒtəbl/
want /wɒnt/
water /ˈwɔːtə(r)/
would like /wʊd ˈlaɪk/
yoghurt /ˈjɒgət/

Consolidation 1

age /eɪdʒ/
boyfriend /ˈbɔɪfrend/
China /ˈtʃaɪnə/
description /dɪˈskrɪpʃn/
herself /həˈself/
live /lɪv/
music /ˈmjuːzɪk/
pop star /ˈpɒp stɑː(r)/

Unit 6

actor /ˈæktə(r)/
advert(isement) /ˈædvɜːt,
  /ədˈvɜːtɪsmənt/
afternoon /ɑːftəˈnuːn/
all over /ɔːl ˈəʊvə(r)/
all round /ɔːl ˈraʊnd/
always /ˈɔːlweɪz/
appetite /ˈæpɪtaɪt/
arrive /əˈraɪv/
baseball /ˈbeɪsbɔːl/
beautiful /ˈbjuːtɪfl/
boutique /buːˈtiːk/
breakfast /ˈbrekfəst/
bring /brɪŋ/
buy /baɪ/
cards /kɑːdz/
cameraman /ˈkæmrəmæn/
carnival /ˈkɑːnɪvl/
clock /klɒk/
colourful /ˈkʌləfl/
company /ˈkʌmpəni/
competition /kɒmpəˈtɪʃn/
concert /ˈkɒnsət/
costume /ˈkɒstjuːm/
dancer /ˈdɑːnsə(r)/
day /deɪ/
designer /dɪˈzaɪnə(r)/
every /ˈevri/
exciting /ɪkˈsaɪtɪŋ/
exercise (sport) /ˈeksəsaɪz/
forget /fəˈget/
get /get/
go /gəʊ/
guitar /gɪˈtɑː(r)/
half /hɑːf/
hat /hæt/
hear /hɪə(r)/
homework /ˈhəʊmwɜːk/
hopeless /ˈhəʊpləs/
hour /ˈaʊə(r)/
huge /hjuːdʒ/
hungry /ˈhʌŋgri/
interesting /ˈɪntrəstɪŋ/
interview /ˈɪntəvjuː/
jacket /ˈdʒækɪt/
last /lɑːst/
late /leɪt/
lesson /ˈlesn/
lunch /lʌntʃ/
million /ˈmɪljən/
musician /mjuːˈzɪʃn/
never /ˈnevə(r)/
newspaper /ˈnjuːspeɪpə(r)/
night /naɪt/
noisy /ˈnɔɪzi/

often /ˈɒfn, ˈɒftən/
party /ˈpɑːti/
past (prep) /pɑːst/
pay for /ˈpeɪ fɔː(r), fə(r)/
plane /pleɪn/
price /praɪs/
producer /prəˈdjuːsə(r)/
quarter /ˈkwɔːtə(r)/
remember /rɪˈmembə(r)/
road /rəʊd/
relaxation /riːlækˈseɪʃn/
(go) shopping /(gəʊ) ˈʃɒpɪŋ/
sing /sɪŋ/
sound (v) /saʊnd/
special offer /speʃl ˈɒfə(r)/
specialize /ˈspeʃəlaɪz/
sport /spɔːt/
sports centre /ˈspɔːts sentə(r)/
stall /stɔːl/
start /stɑːt/
stay /steɪ/
stop /stɒp/
studio /ˈstjuːdiəʊ/
swimmer /ˈswɪmə(r)/
(go) swimming /(gəʊ)
  ˈswɪmɪŋ/
table tennis /ˈteɪbl tenɪs/
take /teɪk/
take place /teɪk ˈpleɪs/
talk /tɔːk/
terrible /ˈterəbl/
them /ðem/
(on) tour /(ɒn) ˈtʊə(r)/
travel /ˈtrævl/
until /ənˈtɪl/
upwards /ˈʌpwədz/
us /ʌs/
usually /ˈjuːʒʊəli/
visit /ˈvɪzɪt/
wait /weɪt/
wash (... away) /wɒʃ (...
  əˈweɪ/
wear /weə(r)/
weekend /wiːˈkend/
win /wɪn/
world /wɜːld/

Unit 7

area /ˈeəriə/
behind /bɪˈhaɪnd/
between /bɪˈtwiːn/
boss /bɒs/
bottle /ˈbɒtl/
children /ˈtʃɪldrən/
circle /ˈsɜːkl/
clever /ˈklevə(r)/
close (v) /kləʊz/
control /kənˈtrəʊl/
crew /kruː/
direction /dəˈrekʃn, dɪ-, daɪ-/
Earth /ɜːθ/
electricity /ɪlekˈtrɪsəti/

feet /fi:t/
few (a ...) /fju:/
garden /'gɑ:dn/
in front of /ɪn 'frʌnt əv/
invention /ɪn'venʃn/
knives (sing. = knife) /naɪvz (naɪf)/
library /'laɪbrəri/
little (a ...) /'lɪtl/
lose /lu:z/
matches /'mætʃɪz/
microphone /'maɪkrəfəʊn/
move /mu:v/
Never mind! /'nevə maɪnd/
No way! /nəʊ 'weɪ/
ocean /'əʊʃn/
off /ɒf/
panel /'pænl/
part /pɑ:t/
play /pleɪ/
produce (v) /prə'dju:s/
put /pʊt/
receive /rɪ'si:v/
rectangle /'rektæŋgl/
round /raʊnd/
salad /'sæləd/
screen /skri:n/
section /'sekʃn/
send /send/
shape (n) /ʃeɪp/
ship /ʃɪp/
size /saɪz/
solar /'səʊlə(r)/
something /'sʌmθɪŋ/
space station /'speɪs steɪʃn/
square (n & adj) /skweə(r)/
string /strɪŋ/
Sun /sʌn/
sunny /'sʌni/
teeth /ti:θ/
tin (n) /tɪn/
tin-opener /'tɪn əʊpnə(r)/
toy /tɔɪ/
triangle /'traɪæŋgl/
triangular /traɪ'æŋgjʊlə(r)/
wheel /wi:l/
wood /wʊd/

Unit 8
aerobics /eə'rəʊbɪks/
air /eə(r)/
agree /ə'gri:/
angry /'æŋgri/
anything /'eniθɪŋ/
athlete /'æθli:t/
athletics /æθ'letɪks/
badminton /'bædmɪntən/
become /bɪ'kʌm/
bicycle /'baɪsɪkl/
blow (v) /bləʊ/
bubble-gum /'bʌbl gʌm/
call (v) /kɔ:l/

can / can't /kæn (kən), kɑ:nt/
centimetres / cm /'sentimi:təz/
champion /'tʃæmpiən/
dangerous /'deɪndʒərəs/
dead /ded/
diameter /daɪ'æmətə(r)/
dive /daɪv/
drum (n) /drʌm/
east /i:st/
enough /ɪ'nʌf/
equipment /ɪ'kwɪpmənt/
fast /fɑ:st/
first (thing) /fɜ:st (θɪŋ)/
fly (v) /flaɪ/
Friday /'fraɪdeɪ/
get a move on /get ə 'mu:v ɒn/
gym /dʒɪm/
habit /'hæbɪt/
Hang on (a minute)! /'hæŋ ɒn (ə mɪnɪt)/
horse /hɔ:s/
judo /'dʒu:dəʊ/
kilometres per hour /kɪ'lɒmɪtəz, 'kɪləmi:təz pər 'aʊə(r)/
laugh /lɑ:f/
laughter /'lɑ:ftə(r)/
learn /lɜ:n/
minute /'mɪnɪt/
Monday /'mʌndeɪ/
must /mʌst, məs/
open /'əʊpən/
out /aʊt/
organize /'ɔ:gənaɪz/
perhaps /pə'hæps/
piano /pi'ænəʊ/
practise /'præktɪs/
regularly /'regjələli/
relax /rɪ'læks/
ride /raɪd/
run /rʌn/
sleep /sli:p/
speak /spi:k/
study /'stʌdi/
Sunday /'sʌndeɪ/
supper /'sʌpə(r)/
sure /ʃʊə(r)/
technique /tek'ni:k/
... think so /θɪŋk səʊ/
Thursday /'θɜ:zdeɪ/
timetable /'taɪmteɪbl/
top /tɒp/
track (running ...) /træk/
train (v) /treɪn/
Tuesday /'tju:zdeɪ/
walk /wɔ:k/
Wednesday /'wenzdeɪ/
week /wi:k/
west /west/
wide /waɪd/
without /wɪ'ðaʊt/

Unit 9
beach /bi:tʃ/
boat /bəʊt/
break (v) /breɪk/
business /'bɪznɪs/
camp /kæmp/
climb /klaɪm/
cloudy /'klaʊdi/
coast /kəʊst/
comfortable /'kʌmftəbl/
coral reef /'kɒrəl ri:f/
cruise /kru:z/
danger (in ...) /'deɪndʒə(r)/
die /daɪ/
environment /ɪn'vaɪrənmənt/
everything /'evriθɪŋ/
explain /ɪk'spleɪn/
fishermen /'fɪʃəmən/
floor /flɔ:(r)/
grow /grəʊ/
happen /'hæpn/
hard (adv) /hɑ:d/
high /haɪ/
immediate, -ly /ɪ'mi:diət, -li/
independent /ɪndɪ'pendənt/
island /'aɪlənd/
kill /kɪl/
metres /'mi:təz/
miserable, -bly /'mɪzrəbl, -i/
mountain /'maʊntɪn/
north /nɔ:θ/
package holiday /'pækɪdʒ hɒlədeɪ/
piece /pi:s/
pollution /pə'lu:ʃn/
raining /'reɪnɪŋ/
sea /si:/
shine /ʃaɪn/
skiing /'ski:ɪŋ/
slope /sləʊp/
slow, -ly /'sləʊ, -li/
snow /snəʊ/
soon /su:n/
south /saʊθ/
stand /stænd/
steady, -ily /'stedi, -əli/
tent /tent/
thousand /'θaʊzənd/
through /θru:/
tour guide /'tʊə gaɪd/
tourist /'tʊərɪst/
traveller /'trævlə(r)/
warm /wɔ:m/
weather /'weðə(r)/
wet /wet/
What's going on? /wɒts gəʊɪŋ 'ɒn/
windy /'wɪndi/
wonderful /'wʌndəfl/

Unit 10
April /'eɪprəl/
at the moment /ət ðə 'məʊmənt/
(on) average /(ɒn) 'ævrɪdʒ/
August /'ɔ:gəst/
birthday /'bɜ:θdeɪ/
biscuit /'bɪskɪt/
(a) bit /ə 'bɪt/
brilliant! /'brɪliənt/
cake /keɪk/
couch potato /kaʊtʃ pə'teɪtəʊ/
date (day) /deɪt/
December /dɪ'sembə(r)/
diet /'daɪət/
fat /fæt/
February /'febrʊəri/
give /gɪv/
go out /gəʊ 'aʊt/
height /haɪt/
How many? /'haʊ meni/
How much? /'haʊ mʌtʃ/
increase (n) /'ɪŋkri:s/
January /'dʒænjʊəri/
July /dʒu:'laɪ/
June /dʒu:n/
just /dʒʌst, dʒəst/
leave /li:v/
length /leŋθ/
Lucky you! /lʌki 'ju:/
magazine /mægə'zi:n/
March /mɑ:tʃ/
May /meɪ/
month /mʌnθ/
November /nəʊ'vembə(r)/
occasion /ə'keɪʒn/
October /ɒk'təʊbə(r)/
per cent /pə 'sent/
pocket money /'pɒkɪt mʌni/
reason /'ri:zn/
second /'sekənd/
September /sep'tembə(r)/
shy /ʃaɪ/
spend (on) /spend (ɒn)/
sweets /swi:ts/
third /θɜ:d/
ticket /'tɪkɪt/
(tell the) truth /(tel ðə) tru:θ/
way /weɪ/
weight /weɪt/

Consolidation 2
billiards /'bɪliədz/
chess /tʃes/
cricket /'krɪkɪt/
double /'dʌbl/
horse-riding /'hɔ:s raɪdɪŋ/
(musical) instrument /(mju:zɪkl) 'ɪnstrəmənt/
omelette /'ɒmlət/
once /wʌns/
survey /'sɜ:veɪ/
unusual /ʌn'ju:zʊəl/

Unit 11

across /ə'krɒs/
alive /ə'laɪv/
both /bəʊθ/
building /'bɪldɪŋ/
clear (adj) /klɪə(r)/
completely /kəm'pli:tli/
damage /'dæmɪdʒ/
emergency /ɪ'mɜ:dʒənsi/
enormous /ɪ'nɔ:məs/
experience /ɪk'spɪəriəns/
extremely /ɪk'stri:mli/
freezing /'fri:zɪŋ/
frightened /'fraɪtənd/
heavy /'hevi/
hope /həʊp/
hospital /'hɒspɪtl/
inside /ɪn'saɪd/
lovely /'lʌvli/
meeting /'mi:tɪŋ/
middle /'mɪdl/
mystery /'mɪstri/
navy /'neɪvi/
over /'əʊvə(r)/
passport /'pɑ:spɔ:t/
race (competition) /reɪs/
ready /'redi/
rescue /'reskju:/
safe /seɪf/
signal /'sɪgnəl/
spy /spaɪ/
stand up /stænd 'ʌp/
still (adj) /stɪl/
storm /stɔ:m/
strange, -ly /'streɪndʒ, -li/
strong /strɒŋ/
suddenly /'sʌdənli/
terrifying /'terɪfaɪɪŋ/
thirsty /'θɜ:sti/
tired /'taɪəd/
typhoon /taɪ'fu:n/
upside-down /ʌpsaɪd 'daʊn/
violent /'vaɪələnt/
wave /weɪv/
yesterday /'jestədeɪ/
zoo /zu:/

Unit 12

accident /'æksɪdənt/
after /'ɑ:ftə(r)/
ago /ə'gəʊ/
airport /'eəpɔ:t/
argument /'ɑ:gjəmənt/
arrest (v) /ə'rest/
back /bæk/
because /bɪ'kɒz, bɪ'kʊz/
(on) board /(ɒn) bɔ:d/
bomb /bɒm/
break (n = rest) /breɪk/
brush /brʌʃ/
bus-stop /'bʌstɒp/
circus /'sɜ:kəs/

clean (v) /kli:n/
decide /dɪ'saɪd/
diary /'daɪəri/
disaster /dɪ'zɑ:stə(r)/
end /end/
finally /'faɪnəli/
flat (n) /flæt/
hangman /'hæŋmæn/
headache /'hedeɪk/
hero /'hɪərəʊ/
hijack /'haɪdʒæk/
horrible /'hɒrəbl/
job /dʒɒb/
jump /dʒʌmp/
lift /lɪft/
news /nju:z/
next /nekst/
passenger /'pæsɪndʒə(r)/
president /'prezɪdənt/
report /rɪ'pɔ:t/
return /rɪ'tɜ:n/
seat (n) /si:t/
search /sɜ:tʃ/
show /ʃəʊ/
squid /skwɪd/
Switzerland /'swɪtsələnd/
theme park /'θi:m pɑ:k/
undersea /ʌndəsi:/
van /væn/

Unit 13

adventure /əd'ventʃə(r)/
against /ə'genst/
amount /ə'maʊnt/
aqualung /'ækwəlʌŋ/
architect /'ɑ:kɪtekt/
attack (v) /ə'tæk/
believe /bɪ'li:v/
born (was ...) /bɔ:n (wɒz, wəz)/
chief /tʃi:f/
cookie /'kʊki/
court (law ...) /kɔ:t/
critic /'krɪtɪk/
death /deθ/
director /də'rektə(r), dɪ-, daɪ-/
edit /'edɪt/
escape /ɪ'skeɪp/
explore, -er /ɪk'splɔ:r, -ə(r), -rə(r)/
farmer /'fɑ:mə(r)/
fight (fought) /faɪt (fɔ:t)/
filmscript /'fɪlmskrɪpt/
fluent, -ly /'flu:ənt, -li/
free time /fri: taɪm/
greedy /'gri:di/
hate /heɪt/
helpful /'helpfl/
hit (n = success) /hɪt/
hostel /'hɒstəl/
hunt, -er /'hʌnt, -ə(r)/
ill /ɪl/

instead /ɪn'sted/
interest (n) /'ɪntrest/
lawyer /'lɔɪə(r)/
lazy /'leɪzi/
movie (... camera) /'mu:vi (kæmrə)/
nowhere /'nəʊweə(r)/
nuclear test /nju:klɪə 'test/
office /'ɒfɪs/
oxygen /'ɒksɪdʒn/
packet /'pækɪt/
pain /peɪn/
period /'pɪəriəd/
poet, -ry /'pəʊɪt, -ət, -ətri/
politician /pɒlə'tɪʃn/
prize /praɪz/
promise /'prɒmɪs/
silence /'saɪləns/
sink (sank) /sɪŋk (sæŋk)/
still (adv) /stɪl/
survive /sə'vaɪv/
underwater /ʌndə'wɔ:tə(r)/
watch (n) /wɒtʃ/
writer /'raɪtə(r)/

Unit 14

book (v = reserve) /bʊk/
blouse /blaʊz/
complete /kəm'pli:t/
Cool! /ku:l/
expedition /ekspə'dɪʃn/
gallery /'gæləri/
history /'hɪstri/
How about ...? /'haʊ əbaʊt/
invitation /ɪnvɪ'teɪʃn/
Jamaica /dʒə'meɪkə/
let's /lets/
market /'mɑ:kɪt/
model /'mɒdl/
North Pole /nɔ:θ 'pəʊl/
palace /'pælɪs/
preparation /prepə'reɪʃn/
pull /pʊl/
relative /'relətɪv/
rock (music) /rɒk/
Shall I / we ...? /ʃæl aɪ, wi:/
silk /sɪlk/
theatre /'θɪətə(r)/
travel agent /'trævl eɪdʒənt/
trip (n) /trɪp/
waistcoat /'weɪskəʊt/
wax (... museum) /wæks (mju:ziəm)/
Why don't we ...? /'waɪ dəʊnt wi:/

Unit 15

absolutely /'æbsəlu:tli/
babies /'beɪbɪz/
belong to /bɪ'lɒŋ tu:, tə/
bone /bəʊn/
bracelet /'breɪslət/

briefcase /'bri:fkeɪs/
cage /keɪdʒ/
cap /kæp/
carry /'kæri/
coat /kəʊt/
credit card /'kredɪt kɑ:d/
disappear /dɪsə'pɪə(r)/
dozen /'dʌzn/
fall out of /fɔ:l 'aʊt əv/
false /fɔ:ls, fɒls/
give someone a hand /gɪv sʌmwʌn ə 'hænd/
glasses /'glɑ:sɪz/
hers /hɜ:z/
human /'hju:mən/
mine /maɪn/
one / ones (pron) /wʌn, wʌnz/
ours /aʊəz/
owner /'əʊnə(r)/
plate /pleɪt/
pocket /'pɒkɪt/
(lost) property /(lɒst) 'prɒpəti/
purse /pɜ:s/
push-chair /'pʊʃ tʃeə(r)/
schoolbag /'sku:lbæg/
skeleton /'skelɪtən/
theirs /ðeəz/
umbrella /ʌm'brelə/
underground /'ʌndəgraʊnd/
wallet /'wɒlɪt/
Whose? /hu:z/
yours /jɔ:z/

Consolidation 3

award (n) /ə'wɔ:d/
ballet /'bæleɪ/
bravery /'breɪvəri/
cave /keɪv/
cheap /tʃi:p/
cliff /klɪf/
daughter /'dɔ:tə(r)/
Egypt /'i:dʒɪpt/
fitness /'fɪtnəs/
flower /'flaʊə(r)/
guide /gaɪd/
health /helθ/
opera /'ɒprə/
path /pɑ:θ/
river /'rɪvə(r)/
station /'steɪʃn/
supermarket /'su:pəmɑ:kɪt/
system /'sɪstəm/
transport /'trænspɔ:t/
upset (adj) /ʌp'set/
Zimbabwe /zɪm'bɑ:bwe/